Alexander Begg

Practical Handbook And Guide To Manitoba And The North-West

Alexander Begg

Practical Handbook And Guide To Manitoba And The North-West

ISBN/EAN: 9783741118296

Manufactured in Europe, USA, Canada, Australia, Japa

Cover: Foto ©Andreas Hilbeck / pixelio.de

Manufactured and distributed by brebook publishing software (www.brebook.com)

Alexander Begg

Practical Handbook And Guide To Manitoba And The North-West

PRACTICAL HAND-BOOK

AND

GUIDE TO MANITOBA

AND

THE NORTH-WEST

—CONTAINING—

INFORMATION ON THE FOLLOWING SUBJECTS:

How to get to Manitoba.
The cost of the journey.
Bonding arrangements.
A description of the journey via the lakes and by all rail.
What to do on the way.
Description of Winnipeg.
Its trade, etc., and Real Estate.
Steamboat interests on the Red River.
Trade between U. S. and Manitoba.
The settlement belt and its parishes.
The town of Selkirk.
Portage la Prairie and westward.
The settlements.
The crops of individual farmers.
The electoral divisions.
Crop report for 1876.
Grain and root crops.
Fruits.
Hay and hay grounds.
Water.
Soil.
Game, large and small.
Fish in lakes and rivers.
Apiculture.
Stock raising.
Wool growing.
Dairy produce.

Importation of well-bred stock.
Salt and salt springs.
The rainfall.
The frost.
The seasons.
Healthfulness of climate.
Absence of epidemics.
Weather Record for 1876.
The grasshoppers.
Fencing.
Fuel and timber.
Tree culture on the prairie.
Prairie fires.
Prices of agricultural implements.
Prices of staples in groceries.
Prices of dry goods and hardware.
Prices of furniture and building material.
Manitoba markets.
The roads.
Exportation of Manitoba wheat for Seed.
Necessity for railway communication.
Railway prospects.
Navigation of Lake Winnipeg and Saskatchewan.
The trade of Manitoba.
Statistics of Trade and Navigation.

Banks.
Homestead law.
The reserves.
The Government.
Agricultural Societies.
A comparison of crops.
A description of present settlers.
Educational matters.
Churches and Societies.
Post Offices and mails.
Express and telegraph.
Advice to the immigrant.
The lands in the Province open for settlement.
The different modes of acquiring land in Manitoba and the North West.
Reasons why immigrants should not settle far in advance of settlements.
The demand for mechanical labor and skill.
Future prospects of the North-West.
The country westward.
A comparison between the United States and the North-West.
Statements from several sources and facts to prove the correctness of the pamphlet.

TORONTO:
ROSE-BELFORD PUBLISHING CO.
MDCCCLXXIX.

A PRACTICAL

HAND-BOOK AND GUIDE

TO

MANITOBA

AND THE NORTH WEST.

THE object of this pamphlet is to place before the public an array of facts in as clear and concise a manner as possible, to demonstrate the great advantage possessed by Manitoba and the North-West for intending settlers and capitalists.

One of the first questions likely to be asked in reference to the country is—How can a person get there? and, in the next place—How much will it cost? To these queries we reply as follows:—Taking Toronto as a starting point, you can go by the Great Western Railway, or the Grand Trunk Railway to Detroit; Michigan Central to Chicago; * The Chicago and North Western Railway, and Chicago, St. Paul and Minneapolis Line to St. Paul; the St. Paul and Pacific Railway to St. Vincent, and thence to Winnipeg by the Pembina Branch of the Canada Pacific Railway, just completed. If you prefer rail and water route, you can go by the Northern Railway to Collingwood, the Grand Trunk to Sarnia, or the Great Western to Windsor, and from either of these three places you can take the steamer direct through the Lakes, without transhipment, to Duluth. From that city you take the Northern Pacific

---

*Samuel Beatty, Agent C. & N. W. R'y, Rossin House Block, York St., Toronto.

Railway to Glyndon, and from thence by the St. Paul and Pacific Railway, and the Pembina Branch of the Canada Pacific Railway to Winnipeg.

Parties living along the line of the Canada Southern Railway, can take it to Detroit, and the roads mentioned above from Detroit to St. Paul.

These are the principal routes ; and now a few suggestions to the traveller may prove of service.

When in Toronto, or wherever you may start from, go to the different railway or steamboat offices and see where you can make the best terms for a through passage direct to Winnipeg, and be sure to mark the route indicated on the ticket offered you, so as to judge whether the accommodation will suit the circumstances of your case. If you have animals, household or other goods to bring with you, try, if possible, to make special arrangements for their freight, at a through rate, direct to Winnipeg, and if you succeed in doing so, be sure and get the agreement in writing from the office where you make the contract, so as to render it binding ; also make certain that the office is a responsible one before you complete your bargain.

Where there are several parties travelling together we would recommend them, if they have no special agreement in regard to a through rate for their effects, &c., to club together, and engage a whole car at car rates to Winnipeg. Each individual can then pay his proportion of the amount according to the quantity of effects, &c., he may have in the car, and this plan will be found a great saving in the item of freight.

The railroads allow one man to ride free with car of household goods when the car contains live stock.

Passenger and freight rates will be furnished to any one who will apply personally or by letter to any of the Roads advertising in this guide.

We subjoin the following extracts from letters written at our request by G. B. Spencer, Esq., Collector of Customs in Winnipeg, and J. W. Taylor, Esq., American Consul at the same place, and the information they contain will prove of great service to those who may desire to come to Manitoba, and bring with them their cattle, household goods, or farming implements :—

"I will, however, ad' ! that emigrants from any of the other Provinces of the Dominion, bringing with them any goods other than effects in use, including horses and cattle, &c., &c., must furnish the Customs on arrival here with a certificate and official stamp from some one of the Collectors of Customs at or near their place of departure, that the goods or animals are the manufacture or production of the Dominion of Canada—otherwise they will be treated on arrival here as if imported from the United States, or any other country, not of the Dominion of Canada.

"(Signed)   G. B. SPENCER,

"15th January, 1877."

"U. S. CONSULATE,
"WINNIPEG, January 25th, 1876.

"DEAR SIR,—In response to your communication of the 17th instant, asking what facilities are extended by the Treasury Department to emigrants from Eastern Canada passing through American territory to Manitoba, I transcribe Art. 723 of U. S. Customs Regulations, which embodies the terms of communications made to this Consulate at different periods since 1871.

"Art. 723. Upon due entry and the giving of a proper bond at frontier ports, by parties intending to pass through the territory of the United States to the Province of Manitoba *via* Pembina, of their personal and household effects, including horses, cattle, and waggons, imported for their own use, and not for sale, the articles may be delivered into the custody and control of the party for the purpose of such transportation and exportation, instead of requiring them to be transported over a regularly bonded route. In such cases, Collectors shall cause entry to be made in triplicate, carefully specifying the articles, with quantities, values and duties, one of which shall be transmitted by mail to the Collector at Pembina. Another given to the owner of the goods, to be by him delivered to the said Collector, and the third detained on the files of the Collector at the post of departure. If desired, parties may give a bond without sureties, on depositing the estimated duties with the Collector of the port where entry is made, which deposit shall be returned on presentation of the proper proofs of exportation.

"In view of these regulations, I would advise any intending emigrant to obtain a Consular certificate in Canada, showing items and values of his stock, present the same to the collector of the port of entry in the United States, and then make his special arrangements for transportation to Manitoba—either by giving his bond with citizens of United States as sureties, or his individual bond without security, or depositing the amount of accruing duties. The latter procedure has been very convenient—the Collector's draft to order of emigrant following the receipt of Collector Spencer's (of Winnipeg), landing certificate.

"The fees to American Officials will not exceed five dollars as follows:—

"Consular certificate at the outset of journey from
  Canada $2 50
"Entry for immediate transportation in bond to
  Manitoba. 1 50
"Inspection, &c., at Pembina 1 00

                                              $5 00

"After passing the United States frontier, the emigrant may take any route he chooses : but I would advise that he should remain in possession of his effects until his arrival in Manitoba. He should understand, however, that his bond will not be released or the duties refunded, if he disposes of any portion of his stock (unavoidable casualties, to be fully explained, excepted), in transit through the United States.

"I am &c.,
"(Signed) J. W. TAYLOR,
"U. S. Consul."

If you intend taking your team with you and driving from Moorhead over the prairie to Winnipeg, you would do well to provide yourself with the following articles, if you do not happen to have them:—

A Tent.	Tin cups.
Frying pan.	Tin plates.
Kettle to boil water.	Knives and forks,(common).
Tea pot.	Iron spoons.
Water pail.	Some wrought nails.
Axe.	A piece of leather (strong),
Hatchet.	paper of wrought tacks, some
Butcher knife.	stout twine.
One or two plough lines and Bedding.	

And your provisions as follows :

Tea.	Ham, bacon or pork.
Sugar.	Flour.
Salt.	Baking Powder.
Pepper.	Butter.
Biscuits.	Matches.

Some Pain-Killer in case of sickness.

Get hobbles* made for your horses to prevent their straying away from you at night. When travelling make it a rule to

---

* Hobbles are straps made to confine the fore feet of the horse to prevent his galloping away. These straps are fastened on just over the hoof above the fetlock, the legs being allowed a play of about a foot apart. In this way the animal can only hop along and cannot consequently travel any distance during the night. Hobbling horses does not in the least interfere with their feeding.

start as early as possible in the morning, take long rests in the middle and heat of the day, and travel again in the cool of the evening so as not *to wear out your horses*.

It is always desirable and in fact necessary for you to take a supply of o... ...m Moorhead, to feed your horses on the way, as grass is not sufficient to keep animals in good condition, where they have to travel day after day with loads. There is, however, pasture all along the road from Moorhead to Winnipeg. In order to camp at the best spots for water and wood, your plan is to enquire, as you go, at the different stage stations along the road, as the men in charge of them will give you all the information you desire. While you keep along the river you are all right, but at some places you have to make a detour and depend upon small lakes and creeks for water; and, as some of them are salty, if your horses should drink at them they would probably become sick, and it is for this reason we advise you to enquire at the stations for the best camping grounds.

With regard to the cost of travelling to Manitoba, we have given a list of rates, but we have done so merely to give some idea of the expense, and would advise parties to make their own terms with the cheapest line.

In reference to this subject, we clip the following from the Winnipeg *Free Press* of the 11th, which may be information to some of our readers :

" Immigration Rates.—Mr. John Ralston has been offered through passenger rates from Montreal to Winnipeg for next season at $18, or to Duluth for $8.40 per 100 lb. for freight ; horses, $10 and cattle $8, to the last mentioned point. The route is from Montreal to Hamilton by boat, thence to Southampton by Great Western Railway, and thence to Duluth by boat, then by Northern Pacific and Red River boats to Winnipeg."

We are informed that the Beatty and Windsor line of steamers, plying to Duluth have combined under the name of the North-west Company, with headquarters at Sarnia. This line will be an extra strong one, and doubtless parties will be able to effect good arrangements with them for transportation.

The third question which is likely to be asked is " What sort of a trip is it to Manitoba ?"

Our reply is as follows :—If you take the steamer either at Collingwood or Sarnia, you will find the boats commodious and comfortable, and the officers, as a rule, most attentive to their passengers. The scenery along the north side of Lake Superior is very fine, and you will have opportunities while the boat is wooding, and receiving or discharging freight, of enjoying yourself fishing, bathing and scrambling about the shore picking up pebbles, mosses and curiosities. To any one in poor health, nothing is so apt to bring the roses to the cheeks as the clear bracing atmosphere of the lakes, especially that of Superior. Parties must bear in mind, however, that the weather during the first trip or two of these Lake Superior steamers is apt to be rather cold, and they should prepare themselves accordingly. Our description applies to later in the season. The passage to Duluth through the lake consumes about three or four days, unless you are detained by bad weather, which will not be very often, as the boats are seaworthy, and do not put in for every slight storm. The time, however, passes so pleasantly, that it is hardly felt, and on the arrival of the boat at Duluth, the almost universal feeling amongst the passengers, is regret at the termination of the voyage. The accommodation for the second-class passengers is very good, and every attention is paid to their comfort. The first thing you do on arriving at Duluth, is to go to the Custom House, and present your papers through a broker (whose office you will easily find), so as to facilitate the forwarding of your effects, if you have more than ordinary baggage. As a rule, freight is forwarded on the Northern Pacific Railway without delay, but if there is any appearance of your goods and chattels being neglected or left behind, apply to the agent of the steamboat company, or to the captain of the boat you arrived in to interfere in the matter. We would here refer you to what we have already said in regard to several parties clubing together and hiring a car, so as to cheapen the rate of freight between Duluth and Moorhead.

Duluth is situated on the side of a high and steep hill at the extreme western end of Lake Superior, and is possessed of a good harbour. It has a very scattered appearance at present, but is destined without doubt to become in time a place of great importance. As you leave it on the cars of the Northern Pacific Railway, you pass through a very mountainous country, nothing but rocks and pine being visible, and you cross several bridges of immense height spanning deep ravines between the mountains. Gradually, however, you come to a prairie country which does not strike the eye as being very productive, the soil being too sandy in many places, and in others covered with great quantities of stones. The land along the Northern Pacific R. R. is thinly settled, and we fear it will be long ere its population will increase to any great extent. The rapid growth, however, of some of the towns along the line, through the instrumentality of the railroad company, is remarkable, especially that of Brainard, Moorhead and Fargo, places of only a few years' standing. As you approach the Red River, the soil improves in quality, and indeed, if you take the overland route from Moorhead to Winnipeg, you will find the land along the river side fair, but a mile or two out on the prairie it is little better than a desert in most places. It is astonishing how little really good land there is unoccupied and suitable for successful cultivation in the north-western States. Thus, along the banks of the Red River in Minnesota and Dakota, the good land is confined to a narrow strip on each side of the stream (most of which is already taken up), and out on the prairie it is hardly fit for settlement. You leave Duluth in the morning and reach Moorhead in the evening, but if the Red River steamers *are* running to Crookston; you will have to change cars at Glyndon, and take a branch line of the St. Paul and Pacific R. R. to that place. It will consume the best part of the next day ere you reach Crookston, but when you arrive there you have no further transhipment until you arrive at Winnipeg. You will find the Red River steamers commodious, and the officers courteous and obliging. The meals on board (for which you have to pay extra), are good and substantial, and the berths clean and comfortable. The trip down the river although a little monotonous is not unpleasant, especially as you generally meet some nice people on board, and the officers of the boat vie with each other to make themselves agreeable to their passengers.

If you intend to go overland from Moorhead you will be able to start the day after your arrival, and will experience the novelty of travelling and camping out on the prairie for the next eight or nine days.

The pleasure of travelling over the prairie may be interrupted now and again by mosquitoes and sometimes bad roads, but taking it altogether, it is quite an enjoyable trip. You eat heartily and sleep well, and you have plenty to employ your time in looking after your team, making and striking camp, and cooking meals. Occasionally you will find some shooting, and at some seasons of the year, especially in the spring and in the fall, you will meet with numbers of ducks, pheasants and prairie chickens. It is not improbable that you may come across a deer, a fox, a skunk, or even a bear, but they are not numerous: altogether you will not find the journey irksome, especially if you take care at starting to have everything in proper shape, according to the instructions we have given you.

When you pass through Pembina, at the boundary line between United States and Manitoba, you have to report yourself at the American Custom-House, and be careful to see that your bonds are properly cancelled by the officials before you pass over into British territory. When you cross over into Manitoba, you will have to obtain a clearance from our own Customs officials at West Lynne, after which you may consider yourself free to travel through the British North-West. If the saving of time is an object to you, we would advise you to take the stage—not otherwise, as you travel day and night (a tedious operation), and make the distance from Moorhead to Winnepeg in thirty-six hours.

And now to retrace our steps, we deem it hardly necessary to describe the all rail part of the trip from Toronto *via* Chicago and St. Paul, as it simply means taking your seat in a car to be whirled through the country at the rate of thirty or forty miles per hour. It is the usual meeting of strangers whom you may never see again—the calling out of stations by the brakesman as you pass along—the slamming of doors, and the whir whir of the wheels as you speed past the telegraph poles—catching now and again a glimpse of fertile fields with lazy cattle grazing in them, or rushing through dense forests, or past farm houses and villages, and now and again a passing train. At the stations it is the same bustle and confusion as anywhere else— the towns and cities appear very much alike, and you rush through the country without an opportunity of judging as to its merits or disadvantages. You are pestered by news-boys and squalling children, and now and again your eyes are gladdened by the sight of a pretty face amongst the lady passengers —you get very thirsty, very dusty very sleepy and very tired, and you are glad when your journey is ended, your only satisfaction being that you have got over the distance at a rapid rate.

So now we have said all we can say about the trip, and we again join you as you approach the city of Winnipeg, the future great centre of trade in the North-West.

As you approach by land or by the river, the first objects that arrest the attention are the Cathedral, Convents, and Colleges of St. Boniface on the eastern side of the Red River. Next you see McLane's mill, a large three story building, and Fort Garry, the Hudson's Bay Company post and headquarters, situated on the Assiniboine River, near its mouth ; and beyond lies what appears to be a very large city, somewhat scattered at the edges, but compactly built in the centre, and this is the city of Winnipeg. It is about sixty miles from the boundary line—the custom-house centre for the North-West, and the seat of Government for the Province.

The growth of Winnipeg has been truly wonderful, as will be seen in the following table :—

700 in 1871,
1,600 " 1872,
3,500 " 1873,
5,000 " 1874,

and since then a proportionate increase.

The origin of Winnipeg was caused by its proximity to Fort Garry, the Hudson's Bay Company post, to which a few years back all the settlers had to resort from far and near for their supplies. This induced several free traders to establish stores in the vicinity to catch the stray pennies, and as the hunters and fur traders usually came to the fort twice a year from the

Saskatchewan, Rocky Mountains, and Norway House for their trading outfits, a good deal of trade was picked up from them by these outsiders. The H. B. Company tried in every way (and who can blame them for it), to discourage this independent trading, which was in opposition to them ; but the time of monopoly was drawing to a close, and the small village near the Fort gradually grew in size and importance. The natura advantages of the place, situated as it is at the junction of the Red and Assiniboine Rivers, which connect through Lakes Manitoba and Winnipeg, with the North and South Saskatchewan, reaching to the Rocky Mountains, making it thereby a centre of trade, assisted greatly towards building it up. Stores and dwellings increased in number ; strangers coming to the country made Winnipeg their headquarters, and in 1869 and 1870, during the rebellion, it became the principal scene of the acts caused by that uprising. This brought it prominently before the public of other parts of the world, and its natural advantages soon became acknowledged, for when peace was restored to the country, and Manitoba became one of the Provinces of the Dominion, Winnipeg became its seat of Government. In consequence of this, it was and is the centre for all Government officials, Dominion or Provincial, to transact their business, and all the supplies for the interior have therefore to be taken from it. It was not incorporated until 1873, when it received the right to elect a Mayor and twelve Aldermen for the Civic Government of the place.

Old inhabitants, who held land within the city limits, which they had purchased in by-gone days at comparatively small figures from the Hudson's Bay Company, had their attention suddenly drawn to the value of their real estate. They began by having their properties surveyed into city lots, and fields which had been used only for pasture, were all at once valued at so much per foot, from which time lots quickly increased in price, thus bringing wealth to their possessors.

Some idea of the rate at which Winnipeg city property has increased in value may be gained by the following instances, being one or two of many such cases :

One lot on Main Street, which could have been purchased in 1871 for $500, is now held at $6,000, a small one story building on it being valued at about $500. $5,000 was refused for this property during the past year. Another corner of Main and Thistle Streets was sold for $500 and is now worth $10,000, and the returns from it warrant the value.

Winnipeg as it stands at present and what it was five years ago, are certainly two very different things ; but as we are more interested in the city of to-day than the hamlet of yesterday, we will deal with the former and leave the latter without further remarks.

The limits of Winnipeg enclose an area of about 2,000 acres or three square miles, and if it goes on at the rate it is now doing, they will soon have to extend the suburbs far beyond where they are at present. The principal thoroughfares are Main Street, which runs the entire length of the city from the Assiniboine River to the northern limits, and Portage Avenue, which commences at Main Street and extends to the western suburbs, each having an almost uniform width of 132 feet. The other streets are 66 feet wide, except Burrows Avenue, which is 99 feet. Main Street can boast of some very fine structures, a few of which we may mention by name, most of them being three story buildings built of brick ; and by the way, we may state here that the bricks manufactured in the neighbourhood of the city are of the very best description and quality, and there can be an unlimited supply of them obtained. But in regard to the buildings, there are first, the Hudson's Bay Co.'s offices ; next, the Canada Pacific Hotel, followed by Hespeler's Block, Custom House, Dominion Land Office, *Free Press* Building, Brown's Store, Ontario Bank, Brouse's Hotel, Schultz Block, Bain & Blanchard's Building, Manitoba Club, Merchants' Bank, Bannatyne's Store, Higgins' Building, Post Office, Ashdown's Hardware Store, Court House, and the City Hall. Besides these there are numerous finely finished frame buildings, presenting quite as tasteful an appearance as their more costly neighbours built of brick. One noticeable fact in regard to the buildings in Winnipeg is, that very few of them, if any, can be called shanties. Going through the city it is most pleasing to observe the neat and tidy appearance of even the meanest of the houses. You see handsome bow windows, fine verandahs, large plate glass panes, and other signs of taste on the part of the owners, but no where will you find the rude cabins so often to be found on the confines of old as well as new cities. There are, it is true, a few of the old log houses still standing, but they look so mean alongside of their more modern neighbours, that their owners are rapidly tearing them down and replacing them by finer buildings.

The streets, as a rule, are all well laid out, and of late the Corporation authorities have not been idle in grading and supplying them with broad side-walks throughout the entire length and breadth of the city. A move is now being made to have the sides of the streets lined with shade trees, which will make Winnipeg one of the handsomest cities west of Chicago. Certain parts of the city have been laid out for public parks, their names and extent being as follows : —

Burrows Park	....	5 acres
Victoria "	....	8 "
Mulligan "	....	3 "

Winnipeg can also boast of one of the finest driving parks in the North-West, with its stands for judges and spectators. The city is thoroughly drained by immense sewers, built something on the plan of the Chicago sewerage, at a cost of over $40,000; and it is proposed, at an early day, to supply the people with as fine clear water as can be found anywhere, from the rise of land up the Assiniboine River. In the mean time, however, as a means for extinguishing fires, there are immense tanks sunk at the corners of the principal streets, which are always kept filled with water, and the city is provided with two Silsby fire-engines, and a first-class hook and ladder apparatus, in charge of an efficient Firemen's Association.

There are, in all, eight churches in the city at present, as follows:—

St. Mary's Church...............Roman Catholic.
Holy Trinity.......................Episcopal.
Christ Church.....................   do
Knox Church.......................Presbyterian.
Grace Church......................Wesleyan Methodist.
Zion Church.......................   do   do
Bethel Church.....................Episcopal   do
Baptist Church.

The educational interests are not forgotten in the St. Boniface College; St. John's College, to which a Ladies' School is to be added in the spring at a cost of $10,000, as well as the Central School, which is contracted for to be built in the spring at a cost of $15,000; Manitoba College, Wesleyan Institute, St. Mary's Academy, and the Common Schools, two in number. The Winnipeg General Hospital is an institution which is well kept up, both by public and private contributions.

In mills and manufactories, the city gives proof of the enterprise of i's people, there being two large flouring mills, three saw mills, four planing mills and sash factories, one foundry, two carriage manufactories, one distillery, one biscuit and confectionery manufactory, and a woollen mill and carriage factory at St. Boniface, besides a number of smaller factories scattered throughout the city.

There are two daily papers, the *Morning Herald* and *Evening Free Press*. There are also two weeklies, the *Free Press* and *Standard*, besides a French paper, *Le Métis*, published at St. Boniface.

There are now over 1,000 buildings of every description within the city limits, and included in that number are several very comfortable hotels, amongst which the principal are:—

The Canada Pacific,
The Grand Central,

The International,
Monchamps,
The Dominion,
Brouse's,

and several others of a minor character.

Along the bank of the river, fronting the city, the scene presented during the summer is one of great activity. The grist and saw mills working night and day, sash factories in full operation, the steamers and barges loading and discharging cargo, and the flat boats moored to the bank unloading their goods—proclaim the fact that Winnipeg is a thriving and prosperous place.

There are now three steamboats plying on the Red River between the Stone Fort and Winnipeg, a distance of almost twenty-one miles, making occasional trips up the Assiniboine to Portage la Prairie, and up the Red River to Emerson on the boundary line. A daily line is also projected for next summer, to run between Winnipeg and Portage la Prairie. The Red River Transportation Company employ seven steamers, and the new line from Moorhead intend building two more, so that will make a total of twelve steamers plying to and from Winnipeg.

The trade of Winnipeg has rapidly developed into a very extensive one, and the city can now boast of several large houses doing business each to the extent of from $100,000 to $250,000 per annum. Of course this does not include the Hudson's Bay Company trade, the Winnipeg branch of which is very great and more than triple that of any of the outside merchants.

In the old days the traders' carts from Fort Garry were accustomed to go as far as Dubuque on the Mississippi for their supplies, they then shortened their trip by going to St. Paul as soon as that city was in a position to furnish them. After this the brigades of carts went only to St. Cloud, when the railway became extended from St. Paul to that place, and to-day the fur traders who used to go to St. Paul for their goods, purchase their outfit in Winnipeg.

Thus the march of commerce has gone on throughout the Western and North-Western States, and as Chicago became the centre of trade in the Western, and St. Paul in the North-Western, so is Winnipeg destined from her position to be the commercial emporium of the British North-West.

In connection with the trade of Winnipeg we quote the following, taken from the St. Paul *Pioneer Press*:

"The trade between the United States and the Province of Manitoba is much larger than is generally supposed. The reporter of the *Pioneer* ascertained incidentally that the Kittson line of steamers on the Red River of the North had carried during the past season over five millions of pounds in bonded goods, or goods which simply passed through the United States to and from Manitoba without undergoing any inspection from subordinate custom house officials. Three hundred car loads of these goods were transferred at St. Paul under the supervision of the customs officers in this city. This fact naturally led the reporter to the office of Dr. Phillips, the Commissioner of Statistics of Minnesota, who, in order to make his forthcoming report as complete as possible, has obtained a schedule of articles shipped into and from Manitoba through the Custom House at Pembina. These articles are, of course, additional to bonded goods, and are simply as are grown, produced or manufactured in the United States or in the Province of Manitoba. Dr. Phillips has appreciated the importance of securing some reliable facts on this important point which seems to have been overlooked by his predecessor in the Statistical Department of the State Government, and hence in his correspondence with Mr. A. E. Nelson, the special deputy collector at Pembina, he has received a complete schedule of articles imported into Manitoba during the season of 1870, from the customs district of Minnesota. A glance at this schedule, which appears in full in the report of the Commissioner of Statistics, shows that the aggregate value of these exports is given at $802,400. Manitoba is able to very nearly balance her exports with her imports, the value of the latter being $794,868; or within less than $8,000 of what was paid for the articles brought into the province from the United States. The imports into the Customs District of Minnesota are given as follows by Mr. Nelson, in the schedule forwarded to Dr. Phillips.

"Value of goods entered for exportation...... $155,361
"Value of free goods entered................ 635,869
"Value of dutiable goods entered for consumption 3,638

"Total imports from Manitoba ... $794,868

"Though the items are not specified in the list of imports, the article of fur is of course the most important production of Manitoba, undressed furs being on the free list. Flour, grain and lumber are also entered free of duty.

"The foregoing facts and figures are interesting, as showing the commercial importance of Manitoba, and of the necessity of completing the lines of communication between St. Paul and Winnipeg. The difficulties of transportation on Red River during the winter are well known, and it only remains for the opening of direct rail communication between the United States and the populous and prosperous regions north of the boundary line, to quicken the trade between Minnesota and Manitoba, into proportions which can now be scarcely estimated.

"It is to be hoped therefore that Dr. Phillips' valuable statistics on this subject may serve to direct attention to the subject, which is worthy of careful consideration on the part of Minnesota legislators, and all other citizens who have an interest in the development and prosperity of the State and the great North-West."

That Winnipeg is to be the centre of competing lines for the carrying trade eastward and westward, there cannot be a shadow of a doubt. Eastward, railways *via* United States, will contend with those through our own territory, and Winnipeg being the junction of the lines, will be the location for the principal depôts.

There are also several local roads projected, the termini of which are to be at Winnipeg; and in the near future, it is not difficult to foresee that a network of railroads westward will be constructed through this vast country, diverging in different directions from one main centre of supply, which from its position and advantages must be Winnipeg. Another point in favour of the city is, that she has the start already in wealth and influence, two very powerful auxiliaries; and although there will doubtless be other cities and towns established in the North-West, yet she will hold the first place and will be in fact the great feeder of the country.

In regard to the future trade of Winnipeg, one has only to look at the immense country opening up westward to the Rocky Mountains which will have to be supplied, to form an idea of what that trade is likely to be. One more word in connection with the future metropolis of the North-West and we say it for the purpose of claiming the attention of capitalists to the splendid field here open for investments. Real estate, as we have already shown, has rapidly increased in value in Winnipeg during the past few years, and lots in the city are bringing fair prices, present value; but there is not the least doubt that even the highest priced lot in the city will more than quadruple its value in the course of the next five or ten years. There are, however, opportunities of buying city property in what is now known as the suburbs, for comparatively low figures, and it is to these especially we would like to draw attention. The present suburbs will, without doubt in a few years, become more central as the city extends its limits, and the value of what are now considered suburban lots will increase to a wonderful extent. Of course the more central the more valuable will be the property, but an investment in Winnipeg city property of to-day, if held a few years, will tell the same tale as investments in Montreal, Toronto, Hamilton, Chicago, Milwaukee and St. Paul have done before in their day. It is well known that parties who purchased real estate in these cities in their early days and held it, lived to see it the source of great wealth to themselves and their children after them.

And now, turning our steps from the city to the country, we will take a cursory view of the Province ere we go into details as to its advantages and resources.

GENERAL DESCRIPTION OF THE PROVINCE.

The main highway, by which you enter the Province at West Lynne, on the American Boundary line, runs northward along the western side of the Red River. A branch office of the Canadian Custom House at Winnipeg has been established at West Lynne, where you have to report your arrival and pass the necessary entries, and you will find the officer in charge (Mr. Bradley), a most accommodating official, who will give you every assistance in his power. The steamers from the United States all stop here, and if you are a passenger on board with your effects, you have nothing to do, as the clerk of the boat reports his manifest, but your personal luggage will have to be examined by the landing waiter, the same as at any other port of entry in the Dominion.

At West Lynne there is a Hudson's Bay Company Post with stores, &c., and shortly afterwards you come to a ferry which connects with the Town of Emerson on the opposite bank of the river. This latter place is in a most flourishing condition, and bids fair to become a large city in the near future. Its inhabitants are enterprising and liberal, and its position as the terminus of the Pembina Branch of the Canadian Pacific Railway, will undoubtedly make it a place of importance. Already, it can boast of several fine buildings, amongst which are one or two churches, hotels, and several handsome stores. And the houses generally, as in Winnipeg, are all of a superior kind, no shanties being visible. There is also a Dominion Lands office established there for the convenience of intending settlers, taking up land in the neighborhood.

Before going further, I will now give you a short outline of the Red River, from West Lynne, until it empties into Lake Winnipeg. From the southern boundary of the Province, till you reach the lake, it is 104 miles in a direct line, but the river is very winding in its course, which more than doubles the distance by water. The average width of the stream is 300 feet, and the banks are from twenty to thirty feet in height, until you reach the low and marshy district in the neighbourhood of Lake Winnipeg. It is navigable to vessels of light draught the entire distance, the only trouble some places being in the parishes of St. Norbert and St. Andrews, where it is very shallow, with slight rapids and boulders in the bed of the stream. It will neither be a difficult nor an expensive matter to entirely remedy this evil, and of late years much has been done by the Government and private enterprise towards that object. The banks on both sides of the river are lined with wood, chiefly poplar, tamarac and a mixture of oak, elm, and birch. Between West Lynne, and the parish of St. Andrews, north of the City of Winnipeg, the woods appear heavier and more continuous on the eastern side of the river than on the western, and beyond this forest line to the eastward and to the westward the vast prairie extends as far as the eye can reach, dotted here and there on the bluffs, and along the numerous creeks, with groves of trees.

The prairie, as a general rule, is level, although in some parts it is slightly undulating, and everywhere it has an inclination towards the river. The soil varies slightly in some parts of the Province, but is chiefly of an alluvial black argillaceous mould, rich in organic deposit, and rests at a usual depth of two and a-half feet on the prairie, and from two and a-half feet to twenty feet on bottom lands. There are swamps and marshes here and there, but on examination they will be found to possess a firm bottom of alluvial soil, similar to the prairie, and so hard that horses and cattle can wade through them in every direction, and as they are generally at a much higher level than the streams, the channels of which are deep, it will not be a difficult matter to drain them so as to bring them under cultivation, when they will prove perhaps to be the finest land in the Province.

Leaving the ferry landing opposite Emerson, you now proceed along a level prairie road, with here and there a deep creek or coolie to cross, keeping at a distance of a mile or so from the river, until you reach the site of the proposed town of Morris, at Scratching River; you meet with very few houses on the way until you arrive at the latter place, where you will find several brick and frame buildings, amongst which are an hotel, school-house, and one or two stores. This is the point of diversion for the Manitoba Southern Railway, which, although at a stand still now, will undoubtedly be built in the near future. When constructed, this railway will run from Winnipeg along the west side of the Red River directly south to Morris, where it will diverge in a south-westerly direction to the neighbourhood of Rock Lake, thus opening up communication with one of the finest portions of the Province, the Pembina mountain district.

After leaving Scratching River, the country gradually appears to be better settled, the houses more numerous, and the land fenced and under cultivation. You now and then pass a tavern or stage station, a church or a-school house, and when you get within about twelve miles of Winnipeg, you lose sight of the prairie altogether, and enter a belt of woods. From this point you meet with small log houses in close proximity to each other, belonging principally to the poorer class of French half-breeds, until you reach "Rivière Salle," where there is a large grist mill belonging to Joseph Lemay, Esq., M.P.P., three stores, a church, a convent, and several fine frame buildings. From this point until you reach Winnipeg, the road continues through the woods, and there is nothing particularly worthy of mention, except that the eastern side of the river appears to be as thickly populated as the western on which you are travelling.

You have now passed four parishes: those of St. Agathe, St. Norbert, St. Vital, and St. Boniface, and when you arrive at the Assiniboine river, you have to pass over on a rope ferry, which lands you within the city limits of the levee and warehouse of the Red River Transportation Company.

You now pass through Winnipeg, and enter upon another of the main highways of the Province. Your course continues to be in a northerly direction along the western side of the Red River, and one of the first objects of interest which attracts your attention is St. John's Cathedral, with the Colleges and Bishop's Court in the back-ground. Near here is Redwood Brewery, a fine property adjoining the fur-trading establishment of Hon. Alfred Boyd. As you journey onwards from this point, the thriving condition of the farms along the road, and the high state of cultivation in which they are kept, attest the thrift and comfort of their owners. You pass on the right-hand side, field after field of waving grain, and to the left is the boundless prairie with herds of cattle grazing here and there, proclaiming the wealth of the neighbouring farmers in live stock.

After leaving St. John's Cathedral, the next church you pass is that of the Rev. John Black, in Kildonan Parish, and further on a few miles the Middle church in St. Paul's; near the latter, on the river bank, is a fine grist mill belonging to Mr. H. Pritchard, which turns out very good work indeed. There are also several windmills in operation along the road, and some of the old settlers prefer this primitive mode to that of steam, asserting that it turns out stronger and better flour.

The country, which is open prairie with a belt of wood along the river, and soil similar to that described between Winnipeg and West Lynne, is very much the same all the way until you enter St. Andrew's parish, soon after which you pass into woods, and these continue until you reach St. Peter's Indian Reserve.

In St. Andrew's, there is a fine steam grist mill belonging to E. H. G. G. Hay, and in connection with it the following extract may be read with interest:—

"MANITOBA FLOUR ABROAD.—The following are extracts from a letter received by Mr. E. H. G. G. Hay, of St. Andrew's, from Mr. William Greey, Government Flour Inspector, at Toronto, in reference to samples of flour sent to him by Mr. Hay. It will be seen that the flour is spoken of in the highest terms. Mr. Greey says:—
'Your favour of 28th ult., and sample of flour arrived here on the

c

11th instant. The flour is an excellent first class "strong bakers," a tip top quality. It beats my standard of that grade. I exhibited the sample on the Corn Exchange yesterday, and it was greatly admired by all the dealers and millers (say twenty or thirty), who saw it, and I invited all I could. The flour is very lively, strong, bright and clearly dressed. It was the impression that such would bring in price $5.25 to $5.30 per barrel. Some "strong bakers" made near here sold for $5.15 a day or two ago. Your spring wheat must evidently be much plumper and stronger than ours of this year, which is unusually thin and poor. Your kind is much needed in wheat or flour if it could be got here safely. You underrated your sample; your kind is much needed in wheat; it is much better than my Government sample of spring extra.'"

There are several stores and taverns along the road in St. Andrew, and two fine churches, and the bank of the river is thickly studded with small log houses the homes of English half-breeds, who do not farm on so extensive a scale as they do in other parts of the Province. Of course there are individual cases of men who farm largely in this part of the country, but they are not numerous. The banks of the river in the neighbourhood of the stone fort are very high, and there are large quantities of stone boulders to be found on the shores and in the bed of the stream, principally limestone.

The stone fort or Lower Fort Garry, consists of about six acres of land enclosed by a high stone wall with bastions at each corner. Inside this enclosure are the Hudson's Bay Company stores and warehouses, and in the centre of the square there is a fine building used for officers' quarters. An extensive farm is also carried on in the neighbourhood, in connection with the fort. A few miles below the stone fort, the new Town of Selkirk is situated at a point where it is expected the Canadian Pacific Railway may cross the Red River. This place has grown wonderfully within the past two years, and it now can boast of the best wharf in the Province, with warehouses, several stores, and a good hotel. There is no doubt, Selkirk will grow to be a large place, as it has a fine country surrounding it, and having secured a start, it is very likely to keep it against any competitors that may arise near it in the future. You now pass into St. Clement's parish, the road being through the woods all the way, until you reach the St. Peter's Indian reserve, where the country gradually begins to decline, until it sinks into swamps and marshes at the mouth of the Red River, where it empties into Lake Winnipeg. The character of the soil along the road we have just travelled, is as follows:—From Winnipeg to St. Andrew's, black loam, after which the land becomes lighter in character, and towards the bank of the river, somewhat mixed with gravel. From St. Andrew's downwards, the soil cannot be surpassed for wheat growing.

The next highway, and perhaps the most important one in

the Province, commences at the City of Winnipeg, and runs in a westerly direction towards Portage la Prairie. It starts along the northern side of the Assiniboine River, first passing through the parish of St. James, which is thickly settled principally by English half-breeds, and the descendants of the pensioners sent out by the British Government in the time of the Hudson's Bay Company. About five miles from Winnipeg, there is the Assiniboine Brewery, a large establishment capable of turning out a fine article of beer, in the manufacture of which they have been lately using the native hop, which grows wild in large quantities in the woods, and can be cultivated to perfection. Beyond the brewery is Silver Heights, and the site of a fine grist mill and distillery which was burnt down a couple of years ago. Silver Heights, the residence of Hon. James McKay, is one of the beautiful spots in the Province. His garden is filled during the summer with vegetables and fruit, amongst which are gooseberries, strawberries, raspberries, currants, red and black, melons, cucumbers, pumpkins, celery, &c., &c., in great profusion.

The aspect of the country, with a few exceptions, is very much the same as along the Red River, the settlement being along the bank of the stream, and on the opposite side of the road open prairie. From St. James you pass into the parish of St. Charles, and from that into Headingly where there are several extensive market gardens, the proprietors of which find a ready sale for their produce in Winnipeg. Here also you will find a comfortable hotel. You now pass into St. François Xavier, which is principally settled by French half-breeds from which you enter Baie St. Paul, also inhabited by the same class of people. In the latter parish there is some of the finest pasture in the Province.

The advantages of this country for cattle-raising on a large scale are demonstrated by the herds of fat cattle seen feeding (12th December) on the nutritious grasses of the wide marsh in the Big Bay. It is a striking fact that cattle prefer the snow-sprinkled marsh grass to the carefully saved hay, oftentimes ; for what reason we have not heard. With the shelter of woods, such food, there is no doubt, would suffice for cattle a great portion of the winter, and, even in the "open," lessening the time required for stable and feeding to a material extent. In fact, we have the experience of farmers in the neighbourhood of the great marshes, to prove that horned cattle may fatten on the marsh grasses up to December, and as early as the 1st of March.

The soil up to this point is the black loam, but we now begin to come to lighter land, which, although it may not last so long as the former, is splendid for wheat-growing and is easier worked. At White Horse plains there is a fine hotel with ample stabling accommodation, and within a mile or so, a H. B. Co. post, in connection with which a large farm is carried on. You now enter Poplar Point, and until that parish is reached, the half-breed reserves monopolize the land outside of the two mile reserve limit; but from its eastern line westward as far as the eye can reach, the country is dotted with comfortable houses and well cultivated fields, exhibiting what the neighbourhood would soon show if the stifling embargo of the reserves were removed. The farmers of this section, as far as the "Beautiful Plains" west of the White Mud River, are mostly from Ontario, and, though sorely tried during the past three years, hope to clear themselves from debt with this year's bountiful crop, and make themselves independent in a few years more. They claim that it is the wheat country "par excellence" of the west; certain it is that their wheat crop of this year was the best, and the grain nearly all No. 1 quality; of many samples of wheat examined by us, shrunk or small grains were the exception, and the yield returned from the thresher better than was hoped for, oats averaging 65 to 70, and wheat somewhat over 30 bushels to the acre. The land along the river continues to be thickly settled through the parish of High Bluff until you reach Portage la Prairie, which is looked upon by many as the future city of this part of the country. We may mention that churches, school-houses, taverns, and stores, are to be met with along the highway at intervals, but there is no necessity for enumerating them. At Portage la Prairie there are two good mills, a branch of Dominion Lands Office, a stage office, and several stores; and taking it altogether, it is quite a lively place. A regular line of stages carrying the mail run between this place and Winnipeg. We have now given a short description of the three principal highways in the Province, running along what is known as the Settlement Belt, and will therefore proceed to a short description of some of the principal outside settlements.

Rivière Salle settlement is best reached by way of Headingly and thence south over the Pembina trail which crosses the Rivière Salle near the upper end of the settlement. Good water can be had by boring to a depth of a dozen or twenty feet. The country is prairie soil, black loam, with numerous coolies or gullies affording good facilities for drainage. Splendid pasturage in the neighbourhood, with good shelter from groves and fringes of woods.

BOYNE RIVER SETTLEMENT.

Township 6, Range 4 and 5 West.

The Boyne River takes its rise in the Pembina mountains, and is about fifty miles long. Its banks are lined with a fringe of heavy oak and elm timber which extends into a forest many miles in extent as you approach the mountains. The soil here, as in the previous settlement, is heavy black loam. This part of the Province is peculiarly adapted for stock-raising, on account of the fine pasturage, water, and protection by timber

POINTE DES CHENES OR STE. ANNE DES CHENES

is situated on the Dawson Road. The country along here has a fine park-like appearance, with large tracts of woods in th vicinity. It has numerous surface springs, and the land is very fertile. In the neighbourhood of Pointe des Chênes there ar the settlements of Clear Spring and Caledonia; the land in both these townships is very rich and well cultivated by the settlers. Plenty of hay, wood, and water in this part of the country.

Springfield Township, 11, Range 4, East, is almost directly north-west of Pointe des Chênes, on the eastern side of the Red River, about four miles north-east of Winnipeg. This locality is well sheltered by a range of hills on the north, and on the east and south by an irregular spur from the same. Water, pure and clear, is obtained near the surface, and hay land and wood in sufficiency.

The soil is so rich and easily worked that, as an intelligent farmer remarked, his farm seemed all ready except the buildings.

SUNNYSIDE.

Township 11, *Range* 5, *East.*

The same remark is applicable to this settlement as to the previous one. It extends to the heavy belt of timber reaching to Lake Superior.

Cook's Creek, Township 12, Range 6, East, is in the same electoral division as Springfield and Sunnyside, and the description of these two townships is applicable also to it. It is well settled.

The electoral division of Rockwood contains the following settlements:

>Rockwood, Township 13, Range 2, East.
>Grassmere, Township 13, Range 1, East.
>Woodlands, Township 14, Range 2, West.
>Victoria, Township 14, Range 2, East.
>Brant, Township 14, Range 1, East.
>Greenwood, Township 15, Range 2, East.
>Dundas, Township 16, Range 2, East.
>Meadow Lee, Township 13, Range 2, West.
>Argyle, Township 14, Range 1, West.

These settlements are in the neighbourhood of inexhaustible quarries of grey limestone, very valuable for building purposes.

The Penitentiary, which is situated in the Township of Rockwood, has been constructed partly of this stone and partly of brick manufactured on the spot. There are also immense deposits of gravel on the ridges. The land of all these settlements is rich prairie with parts heavily timbered. There are abundant surface springs from which excellent water can be obtained, and there are also very fine hay grounds in the vicinity. The railway reserve of the Canada Pacific has retarded the growth of some of these settlements to a certain degree, but not sufficiently so to prevent the district from being one of the most important and flourishing in the Province.

To the north of the Township of Woodlands are the settlements of St. Laurent and Oak Point, on the eastern side of Lake Manitoba, and in connection with this lake we may state the following : The uniform depth is from fifteen to eighteen feet, after passing a short distance from the shore. By far the greater portion of the land bordering on it, especially the south end, is well adapted for settlement, and for the raising of wheat. In many parts the shores are low and marshy at the edges, but which are very valuable for grazing purposes. On the north shore of the lake are innumerable salt springs, from which the natives make a very fine article of salt, and which, if properly worked, would yield largely. Also on the north shore are immense forests of spruce of a gigantic growth, and the waters of the lake are stocked with unlimited quantities of a very superior kind of white fish. The only limestone of any consequence in the Province, west of Poplar Point, is found in inexhaustible quantities on the east and north shores of this lake.

The settlements of Oak Point and St. Laurent are well located, and at the south-western end of the lake, situated near the mouth of the White Mud River (a stream of fine clear water), is the town of Totogan, which aspires to future importance, having about the best harbour on the lake, besides being in the neighbourhood of first-class tillable land, and having good road communication with the eastern portion of the Province. A saw and grist mill, store, hotel, and several houses, have been erected here, and the town is surveyed into lots and well laid out. South of Totogan is the village of Westbourne ; the land in the neighbourhood is of the best quality, and the White Mud River on which it is situated is fringed with oak timber. Westbourne possesses a Church of England, a large hotel, and several stores. The river could no doubt be easily made navigable for schooners and flat-boats, from Lake Manitoba to this point. West of Westbourne is Palestine, probably the largest Canadian settlement in the Province. It is bounded on the west by the White Mud River, and on the north by the "big grass," an immense marsh which is covered along its edges with the very best of hay. Palestine is well wooded with poplar, oak, ash, maple, elm, &c. Wild fruits, such as grapes, plums, black currants, &c., grow in abundance, and the soil is black loam, rather lighter in character than that around Winnipeg, and so fertile, that the farmers who have settled there are astonished at the yield, it being on an average larger than most parts, and equal to any in the Province. Palestine has a flouring mill containing two run of stones, with the most improved machinery, driven by a thirty-five horse power boiler and engine —attached to this mill is a rotary saw-mill, with lath machine, planer, &c. In the immediate vicinity there is a Waterous portable saw-mill, with twenty horse power boiler and engine, capable of sawing 2,000 feet per hour, together with coupling, &c., for running a threshing machine. To the north of Palestine, especially along the Big Grass River, is a fine tract of good land in every way suitable for farming purposes. There is plenty of wood and cold spring water flowing down from the Riding Mountains. To the north-west we soon reach the Riding Mountains, where there is abundance of water and wood and arable land. The country here produces great quantities of plums and other wild fruits.

We must now, however, retrace our steps in the direction of Portage la Prairie, so as to complete our list of the principal settlements.

About half way between Palestine and Westbourne, is the rising settlement of Woodside, which is situated at the second crossing of the White Mud River, and has a post office. The soil is about the same as described in Palestine.

After passing Westbourne on your way to Portage la Prairie, you come to the settlement of Burnside, which is also a very flourishing Township, and contains some of the largest farms in the Province. The land is excellent here, with abundance of hay, wood, and water.

Portage la Prairie we have already mentioned, but we may add here that steps are being taken for placing a splendid mill in operation at this point, the necessity for which may be seen by the following list of crops produced by the farmers in the neighbourhood during the past year.

Dilworth	1,700	bushels.
Alcock	3,000	"
Moss	2,000	"
McKenzie	7,000	"
Grant	4,000	"
Monroe	3,000	"
A. McKenzie	3,000	"
Houir	1,600	"
Gerrard	1,000	"
Brown	2,500	"

Burgess	1,200	bushels.
Cuthbert	1,500	"
Coadman	1,200	"
Wilton	3,000	"
Whimster	3,200	"
Ogletree	1,800	"
Connor	3,200	"
Sissons	2,000	"
Kittson	2,000	"
Bell	5,000	"
Ferris	5,000	"
Meelon	1,300	"
Logan	1,500	"
Mawhinney	2,500	"
	62,200	bushels.

Having now given a short description of some of the principal settlements in the Province, we will subjoin a list according to the late electoral divisions, distinguishing the parishes from the settlements.

1. Lake Manitoba,
    St. Laurent (parish),
    Oak Point.
2. Westbourne,
    Burnside,
    Totogan,
    Woodside,
    Palestine,
    Livingstone,
    Beautiful Plains.
3. Portage la Prairie (parish),
    Oak Land.
4. High Bluff (parish).
5. Poplar Point "
    Ossowa,
    Melbourne.
6. Baie St. Paul (parish),
    Poplar Heights.
7. St. Francis Xavier, East (parish).
8. St. Francis Xavier, West (parish).
9. Headingly (parish),
    Rivière Salle,
    Boyne.

NOTE.—Since writing the above, the Marquette Milling Co. have succeeded in putting their mill at Portage la Prairie in operation, and are turning out a very fine article of flour

10. St. Charles (parish),
    St. Boniface, West (parish).
11. St. James (parish).
12. City of Winnipeg.
13. Kildonan (parish),
    St. John's (parish).
14. St. Paul's (parish).
15. St. Andrew's, South (parish).
16. St. Andrew's, North (parish).
17. St. Clement's (parish),
    Dynover or St. Peter's,
    Town of Selkirk,
    Clandeboye,
    Whitewold.
18. Rockwood,
    Grassmere,
    Brant,
    Victoria,
    Greenwood,
    Dundas,
    Meadow Lea,
    Argyle,
    Woodlands.
19. Springfield,
    Sunnyside,
    Cook's Creek.
20. St. Boniface (parish),
    Notre Dame de Lorette (parish),
    Prairie Grove.
21. St. Vital (parish).
22. St. Norbert "
23. St. Agathe "
    Emerson,
    Hudson,
    Franklin,
    Rivière aux Roseaux,
    Mellwood,
    West Lynne,
    Dufferin,
    Letellier,
    Rivière aux Marais.
    Rivière aux Prunes,
    Rivière aux Gratias,
    Rivière au Rat.
24. St. Anne,
    Ste. Anne des Chênes.
    Clear Spring,
    Caledonia.

And now in order to give our readers an idea of the producing qualities of Manitoba soil, we publish the following reliable statement from the Manitoba *Free Press*, of the 16th September, 1876.

It will be seen by these returns, gathered simultaneously in thirty-four different settlements by intelligent farmers, who in some cases spent days in inspection before summing up their conclusions, that the famous average of Manitoba's growth has been somewhat lessened by various causes, some local and some general, but mostly peculiar to this year. The unusually heavy rains of the late season have done their share, especially on low lands selected last year—an average season; whereas this has been the wettest known since 1869. Another cause by which the average has suffered materially is the sowing on a first ploughing, as done often by new settlers rather than await the slow process of rotting the sod; the half crop grown, is, however, better than none at all, and will go far towards provisioning those settlers' families for the winter. The loss by the depredations of blackbirds in some neighbourhoods suggests an inquiry into a means for their destruction. Another cause strongly felt in some places is from old and deteriorated seed, it being remarked that where new seed was used the difference was easily perceptible.

These returns are interesting also, as showing the remarkable evenness of the productive quality of the land and its capacity for producing what would be considered most surprising returns elsewhere, under such special disadvantages as ruled this season. Just now, when it seems so distinctly marked that the Middle and Eastern States and Ontario are becoming less reliable for agriculture, the endless virgin lands of our North-West are becoming known as specially productive wheat fields, and may be offered to their people for settlement on condition only of building railroads to reach them by.

AVERAGE PRODUCT PER ACRE.

SETTLEMENTS ON RED RIVER.

	Wheat.	Barley.	Oats.	Peas.	Potatoes.	Turnips.
Emerson	25	40	50	25	200	
Whitehaven, (Plum Creek)	35	40	50	35	200	400
Scratching River	25	40	40	25	200	
Union Point	30	50		25		400
St. Vital & St. Norbert	35	45	60	30	100	
Kildonan	30	45	50	30	200	

	Wheat.	Barley.	Oats.	Peas.	Potatoes.	Turnips.
S. St. Andrew's	30	40	45	20	250	
N. St. Andrew	30	30	28	32		
St. Clement's	35	50	55	40	300	
St. Peter's	35	50	55	40	360	

SETTLEMENTS ON THE ASSINIBOINE RIVER.

	Wheat.	Barley.	Oats.	Peas.	Potatoes.	Turnips.
St. James	30	45	50	30	250	
St. Charles	30	40	50	30	250	
Headingly	30	45	60	20	150	100
St. F. Xavier	36	35	50	40		500
Baie St. Paul	40	50	65	40	200	
Poplar Point	35	40	55	22	300	
High Bluff	35	40	55	22	200	
Portage la Prairie	30	40	40	30	250	

SETTLEMENTS ON WHITE MUD RIVER.

	Wheat.	Barley.	Oats.	Peas.	Potatoes.	Turnips.
Totogan	35	45	50	35	400	1000
Woodside	35	40	60	60	400	100
Westbourne	36	40	60	40	150	
Palestine	35		75	25	200	

OUTLYING PRAIRIE SETTLEMENTS EAST OF RED RIVER.

	Wheat.	Barley.	Oats.	Peas.	Potatoes.	Turnips.
Springfield	28	30	45	25	300	700
Prairie Grove	35	50	50	40	350	
Sunnyside and Cook's Creek	35	40	50		200	
Rosseau	30	40	60	30	300	

OUTLYING PRAIRIE SETTLEMENTS NORTH OF ASSINIBOINE RIVER.

	Wheat.	Barley.	Oats.	Peas.	Potatoes.	Turnips.
Rockwood, Victoria & Gressmere	25	52	40	20	250	500
Greenwood	30	40	50	30	350	
Tp. 15, R. I. E	45					
Woodlands and Meadow Lea.	30	35	50	20	200	
Ossowa	20	25	45		140	

OUTLYING PRAIRIE SETTLEMENTS SOUTH OF ASSINIBOINE RIVER.

	Wheat.	Barley.	Oats.	Peas.	Potatoes.	Turnips.
Pembina Mt	35	•	50	20	150	
Boyne River	38	60	60	30	300	

REMARKS.

EMERSON.—Later growth here much retarded by heavy rains, and a local hailstorm which battered grain down; about one-third of the whole area sown on the fresh soil, and produced 18 to 20 bus. per acre.

WHITEHAVEN.—Being a young settlement and crops sown on new ploughed land, this average is very satisfactory.

SCRATCHING RIVER.—Crops mostly on new ploughed land, its average, however, is about 15 to 20 bus. per acre.

KILDONAN.—Loss of average here, owing to rust and mildew; rains very heavy in latter part of season.

S. ST. ANDREW'S.—Wheat light, and all crops shrunken from effect of unusually heavy rains in August.

N. ST. ANDREW'S.—Average below ordinary season. Harvest very wet and trying. Roots will still increase in product.

ST. CLEMENT'S AND ST. PETER'S.—Wheat and barley suffered from wet season, still average will likely be higher than given.

ST. JAMES.—Great loss here from lodging; samples inferior, and somewhat shrunken by extreme wet weather.

HEADINGLY.—Barley and wheat will be poor colour, but all grain heavy. Root crops will yet be good. Peas a comparatively light crop; very wet season.

POPLAR POINT.—Grain did not fill as well as usual. The wettest season known since '59; crops too luxuriant in stalk, but grain heavy.

HIGH BLUFF.—All crops suffered in quantity and colour from heavy and continued rains.

PORTAGE LA PRAIRIE.—Average higher than given; season wet; roots much damaged.

WOODSIDE.—Loss here from blackbirds.

PALESTINE.—Loss of average here by local causes and inferiority of seed.

TOTOGON.—A1 grain, and oats particularly, suffered from blackbirds and lodging by heavy rains.

SPRINGFIELD.—Some injury here by rust from wet harvest, grain very much delayed in ripening.

PRAIRIE GROVE.—Damage by blackbirds and rains.

SUNNYSIDE AND COOK'S CREEK.—Average lessened here by drowning in low lands, and wet harvest. Root crop light.

ROCKWOOD, GRASSMERE AND VICTORIA.—Crops here not up to usual average; considerable grain lodged.

WOODLAND AND MEADOW LEA.—Average five bushels less than would have been in average season. Seed inferior.

OSSOWA.—Most of area sown here newly broken ground, average lessened thereby.

PEMBINA MOUNTAIN.—Less returns on account of large area sown on first plowing, but even then good half crops returned.

BOYNE RIVER.—Blackbirds destroyed one-tenth of the crop. Settlers complain of unoccupied homesteads.

It may safely be assumed, that but for the special causes mentioned, such as heavy rains, old seed, and sowing on new land, the returns of the whole Province would have been one-sixth better. We have collected the averages in divisions of areas separated by the great rivers which have respectively formed the nucleus of settlement and of whose rich valleys this city is the natural marketing centre, as follows :

AVERAGE PRODUCT PER ACRE.

SETTLEMENT ON RED RIVER.—Wheat 32 bushels, barley 42 oats 44½, peas 27¾, potatoes 182, turnips 400.

SETTLEMENT ON THE ASSINIBOINE RIVER.—Wheat 33½ bushels, barley 40¾, oats 53½, peas 29½, potatoes 150, turnips 750.

SETTLEMENT ON WHITE MUD RIVER.—Wheat 35 bushels, barley 40, oats 60, peas 31¼, potatoes 287½, turnips 1,000.

SETTLEMENT EAST OF RED RIVER.—Wheat 29½, barley 40, oats 51¼, peas 32, potatoes 387, turnips 700.

SETTLEMENT NORTH OF ASSINIBOINE.—Wheat 30, barley 9, oats 41, peas 23½, potatoes 235, turnips 700.

SETTLEMENT SOUTH OF ASSINIBOINE.—Wheat 36½ bushels, barley 60, oats 55, peas 25, potatoes 225, turnips 600.

THE TOTAL AVERAGE PRODUCTION

throughout the whole Province of Manitoba this year, will therefore be found to be, as nearly as may be : Wheat 32¼ bushels, barley 42½, oats 51, peas 32, potatoes 229, turnips 662½.

This is a much less total than was expected in the early part of the season; still greater than was latterly looked for, it being feared that the continual rains during the usual term of harvest would have utterly destroyed the crops in many sections.

The figures cited above, together with others in our possession, would indicate the total yields of the Province to be about: Wheat, 480,000 bushels ; barley, 173,000 ; oats, 380,000 ; Peas, 45,000 ; other grains, 5,000 ; potatoes, 460,000 ; turnips and other roots, 700,000.

It has been feared by some that the effect of the bountiful yield will be the reduction of prices below a paying point. However, while prices are sure to range much lower than they have for many years past, we think that next spring, when the immigration, which is sure to pour in, begins, will demonstrate that those who have sold their wheat at much below one dollar a bushel are considerably out. Estimates, based upon importation statistics, place the Provincial and North-West Territorial consumption of flour for the next year at ninety thousand barrels, an equivalent of 360,000 bushels of wheat. This would leave only 120,000 bushels for seed and holding over—plainly insufficient. However, we are disposed to believe that the flour consumption has been slightly over-estimated ; but not so much so as to leave any considerable surplus of wheat after the next twelve months' requirements are supplied. The flour-manufacturing capacity of the Province has been increased by twenty run of stone.

Of the coarse grains the supply will be greater in proportion to the demand, and prices thereof may be expected to range low. But even these we confidently expect to see fairly remunerative, as a large quantity will be consumed in fattening meat for our own market, which hitherto has been supplied, almost entirely, by importation, not for the want of stock so much as the want of grain to bring the same to fair slaughtering condition.

Thus, taking everything into account, it is really doubtful, had we shipping facilities, whether they would be called into requisition for grain exportation even with this year's production on our hands.

Immigration being bound to keep pace with our increasing grain growing, it may be reasonably deduced that long before we have a surplus for exportation eastward we shall be in possession of competing routes of transportation in the Canadian Pacific Railway to Thunder Bay, and the American railway system. Neither is it going too far in the hopeful direction to conjecture that when we have a surplus to export, an abundant and high-priced market will be available in the wants of more southern provinces and states for new and hardier seed. A very high authority on the subject has predicted that for the first ten years of our surplus production it will be exported for seed purposes, and at the expiration of that time the North-West will be known all over the continent as its principal granary for the supply of breadstuffs. In view of the general feeling of joy and congratulation, we think it would be well to proclaim a day of thanksgiving and prayer throughout the Province for the grand results of an abundant harvest.

In addition to the above, we give

A FEW FACTS CONCERNING GRAIN AND ROOT CROPS

IN MANITOBA.

WHEAT.—The average yield is from thirty to forty bushels per acre. Individual cases are known of sixty bushels spring, per acre, and as much as seventy bushels have been produced from one bushel sown.

OATS.—The average yield per acre is from fifty to sixty bushels, although individual cases are known of 100 bushels to the acre.

BARLEY.—Next to wheat, barley is a favourite cereal with the Manitoba farmer; its yield varies from forty to fifty bushels per acre, although as high as sixty bushels have been known. Its weight is from fifty to fifty-five pounds per bushel, and it is an acknowledged fact that the barley of Manitoba is unsurpassed anywhere for brewing purposes, on account of the superior quality and fine colour.

POTATOES are produced to perfection in Manitoba. Their mealy quality, snowy whiteness, and farinaceous properties cannot be excelled anywhere, and the yield is enormous—as high as 600 bushels to the acre—the average being from 400 to 500 bushels.

TURNIPS yield immensely, in some cases as many as 1,000 bushels, and from 500 to 700 being quite common.

CORN.—Indian corn is not extensively cultivated, and it is thought that the large kind cannot be successfully raised, one reason being the cool nights for which Manitoba is noted, and which is beneficial to all other crops except corn, but the smaller description can be profitably grown. Sweet corn succeeds admirably.

Flax and Hemp have been cultivated and grown well, but the want of proper mills caused their cultivation to be almost discontinued.

Grasses all grow to perfection, especially Timothy.

Beets, carrots, and all other root crops come to large growth, and their quality cannot be beaten anywhere. In fact, the Province of Manitoba excels in root crops, and in regard to beet especially, it is looked forward to that the production of this vegetable will in future rise to great importance in connection with the manufacture of beet-root sugar. A large field is open to capitalists in this line.

In garden vegetables and salad plants, we may mention the following as being particularly worthy of notice:—

Cabbages attain enormous size.
Cauliflower   do.
Lettuce, very crisp and fine.
Celery, large and white, with delicious flavour.
Cucumbers grow to a large size.
Melons succeed well in the open air, first started in the hot bed.
Rhubarb succeeds well.
Onions are another speciality in the Province, and yield largely of every variety.
Tomatoes do very well, and the generality of other garden vegetables attain great perfection.

The vegetables, however, that attain the greatest perfection are

Potatoes,   Cabbages,

Onions, Cauliflowers.
Beet,

In conclusion we may quote the following from the Montreal *Herald* in regard to some Manitoba products exhibited in the Corn Exchange of that city:

"The oats were very fine, and the number of stalks growing from one seed showed how productive was the crop. The wild hops rivalled anything of the cultivated class that we have seen, and the peas and broad beans were really splendid. Fancy early rose potatoes, some tubers nine inches long and weighing two pounds, the whole of the selections averaging from 1½ to 1¾ pounds each. Then, there were seedling potatoes of the first year, as large as a good sized hen's egg, and onions—the red and brown sort, from a pound to a pound and three quarters. A twenty-six pounds marble head cabbage is a rather substantial vegetable product, while a red cabbage of ten pounds was also on view. And these are no uncommon things."

In roots and vegetables we would refer our readers to the extract under this class taken from the report of the Manitoba Provincial Show of 1876, and inserted at the end of this book.

The culture of fruit has heretofore been neglected in Manitoba, but lately the attention of nurserymen in the east has been attracted to this country, and several successful efforts have been made to introduce a variety of plants into the Province. There is no reason why apple trees should not be raised in this country, if care is taken at the outset to protect the plants in the spring, and it has been suggested by a writer that all young apple trees should have a wrapping of straw so as to protect them in the spring from alternate thawing and freezing—a great detriment to their growth. It has been proved that apple trees do thrive in this country, and there is no doubt that the celebrated "Fameuse" of Quebec could be produced here to perfection. In Minnesota, not many years ago, it was contended that apple trees would not grow there, and yet to-day the Minnesota apple is a notable product of that State. If Minnesota can produce apples, there is no reason why Manitoba should not do so equally as well.

Wild fruits abound in the Province, amongst which may be mentioned strawberries, raspberries, whortleberries, cranberries, plums, black and red currants, blueberries and grape, so that there is no scarcity of fruit for the settler.

The principal wood in the country is poplar, next to which is oak, and in addition to these are the following:—spruce, tamarac, birch, elm, ash, and maple. All along the rivers and creeks, the banks are lined with woods, and the prairie is dotted with groves which afford a plentiful supply of firewood and fencing for the adjoining settlers. Timber for milling purposes is procured in the vicinity of the lakes, and on the banks of some of the streams, such as Rosseau, Broken-Head river—White Mouth, Birch river, and upper end of the Assiniboine, and at the northern end of Lake Manitoba the pine grows to a very large size, and is of the best description.

The uncultivated portions of the prairie, and the numerous marshes, afford everywhere a plentiful supply of hay which can be had for the gathering by the settler—and water, we have already shown, can be procured almost anywhere, either from the river or creek, or by digging surface wells on the prairie.

The country abounds with game of great variety, consisting of the following kinds:

In the feathered tribe:—

Prairie chickens.	Swans.
Pheasants.	Cranes.
Partridges.	Geese.
Pigeons.	Snipe.
Ducks.	Plover, &c., &c.

In the larger game we may mention:—

Moose,	Mink,
Deer,	Martin,
Antelope,	Otter,
Bear,	Muskrat,
Wolves,	Beaver,
Foxes,	Skunk, and large numbers of

rabbits are to be found in the woods.

The lakes and rivers are filled with fish of the following kinds:—

White-fish,	Perch,
Pickerel,	Suckers, (Red and White),
Pike,	Sun-fish,
Catfish,	Gold Eye,
Sturgeon,	Carp, and in some parts, trout
Rock Bass,	and Maskinonge.
Black Bass,	

The white-fish of Lakes Winnipeg and Manitoba is particularly worthy of mention, as being equal in quality to that found in Lake Superior.

In the woods there are swarms of wild bees to be found, the honey from which is of a very fine quality, and there is no doubt that apiculture can be carried on with great success in Manitoba. The dry air and clear skies, together with the rich flora of the country, afford every facility for remunerative bee culture. A very fine sample of honey was shown by a Mr. Robinson, from the Rosseau, at the Provincial Show of 1876.

Manitoba is destined to become one of the finest stock-raising countries in the world. Its boundless prairies, covered with luxuriant grasses, and the numerous marshes containing the very best feed for cattle, are among the peculiar advantages of the Province for this line of industry. The cool nights for which Manitoba is famous, is a most beneficial feature in regard to stock, and the remarkable dryness and healthfulness of the winter tends to make cattle fat and well conditioned. The easy access to fine water which exists in nearly every part of the Province, is another advantage in stock-raising. The abundance of hay everywhere makes it an easy matter for farmers to winter their stock, and in addition to this there is, and will be for years, a ready home market for beef.

In fact there have been every year heavy importations of live stock from the United States to supply the demand in the Province, simply because our farmers have not heretofore paid sufficient attention to this branch of farming. The usual yield of prairie grass when cut into hay is from three to four tons per acre. It usually grows about five or six feet high, and, although coarse, is very nutritious. Cattle can be wintered without any coarse grain, and keep fat.

It is now over forty years since the introduction of sheep into Red River, and no case of any disease attacking them has ever been seen or heard of. The wool is of a very good quality, and the yield is from six to eight pounds per fleece from wethers, and from 2 to $3\frac{1}{2}$ from ewes. Beef and mutton from Manitoba-fed cattle is very juicy and tender.

There are as yet no cheese factories established here, but there are good openings for that branch of industry, especially as farmers find it very profitable to cultivate stock-raising in conjunction with their other branches of farming. There is a large home demand for butter, which as yet seems never to be fully supplied, and in consequence a great deal has been imported from the United States. We would recommend those who are able, to bring with them well-bred stock, especially bulls and stallions, the better classes of which are scarce in the Province. In fact anything that will tend to improve the stock of any class of domestic animals now in Manitoba, will be a boon to the country generally. Sufficient attention has not been paid to this important matter by our farmers, although there have been individual cases where well-bred animals have been brought in for breeding purposes, the venture having proved remunerative in the highest degree to the enterprising men who undertook them.

In connection with stock-raising, dairy produce, &c., and in conjunction therewith beef and butter packing, we may again refer to the salt springs which exist in parts of the country. The brine from these springs yields almost a bushel of salt to thirty or forty gallons of the water, and the article thus produced is equal to any English, American, or Canadian manufacture. The salt business has not been cultivated as yet to any extent, but in the near future it will certainly become a very important feature of the country, when beef, pork, butter and fish packing is gone into extensively.

The rain-fall of Manitoba is peculiarly favourable to agriculture. In the spring and summer there are refreshing showers at short intervals, and what is termed a dry season is seldom or ever known.

In another part of this pamphlet will be seen a thorough weather record for 1876, by which, however, it will be observed that the year just passed experienced a greater fall of rain than any of the four previous seasons. During harvest time, it seldom happens that farmers are annoyed or put back by wet weather, while during the time the crops are growing their eyes are gladdened by the fresh invigorating showers so peculiar to the country, and this feature of itself is perhaps one of the greatest boons known to the agriculturist.

In the winter the frost penetrates on exposed places to the depth of from three to four feet, that is where the earth is lightly covered with snow. Where it is covered with snow, it is seldom frozen deeper than eighteen inches. Vegetation begins and progresses before the frost is all out of the ground; owing is generally commenced when it is thawed to the depth of six inches, at which time the surface is perfectly dry. It is a fact that this frost helps the growth of crops, owing to the heat of the sun by day causing a continual evaporation from the underlying strata of frost.

The seasons are as follows:—*Spring*—April and May. Snow disappears rapidly, and ground dries up quickly, sowing commences from the middle towards the end of April, and finishes in the beginning of May. *Summer*—June, July, August, and part of September. Weather bright and clear with frequent showers—very warm at times during the day—night cool and refreshing—harvesting commences about the end of August, and ends about the middle of September.

Autumn.—Part of September and October.

Perhaps the most enjoyable season of the year—The air is balmy and exceedingly pleasant. At this period of the year the prairie fires rage, and the atmosphere has rather a smoky appearance, not disagreeable, however.

Winter.—November, December, January, February, March.

In the early part of November, the Indian Summer generally commences, and then follows the loveliest portion of the season, which usually lasts from nine days to a fortnight. The weather warm, the atmosphere hazy and calm, and every object appearing to wear a tranquil and drowsy aspect. Then comes winter, generally ushered in by a soft fleecy fall of snow, succeeded by days of extreme clearness with a steel blue sky and invigorating atmosphere, not too cold. In December the winter regularly sets in and, until the end of March, the weather continues steady, with perhaps one thaw in January, and occasionally snow-storms. The days are clear and bright, and the cold much softened by the brilliancy of the sun.

The winter nights in Manitoba are really splendid, generally with a clear and starlight sky, and when the moon throws her full orbed face towards the earth, the scene is one of peerless grandeur. The cold, as a general thing, is not as much felt by individuals as in Quebec and even parts of Ontario, on account of the stillness of the air and brilliancy of the sun.

We have the testimony of the Honourable Mr. Sutherland, Senator, who has lived in the Province for over 53 years, that he has never known an epidemic in Manitoba. The country places are entirely free from fevers, agues and other ills, and since the City of Winnipeg has been thoroughly drained, there have been few cases of sickness within its limits. Mr. Sutherland also states, that small pox has never been known within the limits of the Province. During the last few months, while that loathsome disease was prevalent amongst the Icelandic settlers on Lake Winnipeg, we of Manitoba have been spared the scourge. For this extreme healthfulness of our country, we have much to thank the Almighty—we consider this healthful state of the climate of Manitoba as of paramount importance to the farmer, for what to him are fair fields and meadows, beautiful crops and the acquisition of wealth, if to attain them he is obliged to sacrifice his own health and that of his family. The dryness of the air, the character of the soil, which retains no stagnant pools to send forth poisonous exhalations, and the almost total absence of fog or mist; the brilliancy of the sunlight; the pleasing succession of its seasons, all combine to make Manitoba a climate of unrivalled salubrity, and the home of a healthy, prosperous, and joyous people.

The following is the weather record for 1876, carefully prepared by James Stewart, Esq., signal observer at Winnipeg.

GENERAL METEOROLOGICAL REGISTER FOR 1876.

Observed at Winnipeg, Manitoba, Lat. 49 deg. 52 min., N., Long. 97 deg. 08 min., W. from Greenwich. Height above the sea, 754 feet.

By JAMES STEWART, Signal Observer.

PHENOMENA.	Jan.	Feb.	March.	April.	May.	June.	July.	Aug.	Sept.	Oct.	Nov.	Dec.
Mean monthly temperature	—4.33	—6.47	8.90	35.90	52.84	60.02	66.56	63.80	52.58	37.16	14.76	—5.64
Highest temperature	36.0	32.0	37.6	74.6	90.0	92.0	94.5	96.0	75.5	68.0	63.6	28.5
Lowest temperature	—35.0	—43.0	—22.5	3.2	27.0	30.0	39.0	31.5	39.0	15.0	—32.3	—38.3
Mean barometric pressure	29.190	29.275	29.309	29.099	29.015	29.015	29.059	29.053	29.130	29.023	29.259	29.242
Mean humidity of the air	91	95	87	78	71	74	78	86	89	82	87	90
Mean elasticity of aqueous vapour	.042	.038	.061	.176	.203	.401	.530	.540	.371	.190	.086	.032
Mean amount of sky clouded	.40	.40	.48	.43	.49	.43	.37	.46	.47	.55	.65	.45
Velocity of wind (miles per hour)	7.02	7.46	6.60	9.58	9.67	10.16	6.45	9.52	7.98	10.47	8.14	8.90
Total amount of rain	0	.0	0	0.460	2.850	5.400	3.315	9.440	1.360	0.130	0	0
Total amount of snow	10.36	13.20	9.26	1.80	2.90	0	0	0	0	5.32	24.69	7.18
Number of auroras	1	6	5	2	2	0	1	4	6	2	1	1
Number of thunder storms	0	0	0	1	4	5	5	8	1	0	0	0

MISCELLANEOUS PERIODICAL PHENOMENA.

The warmest day during the year was 31st July, the mean temperature being 81.50.

The coldest day during the year was the 1st February, the mean temperature being —30.95.

The highest reading of the thermometer was 95.0 on the 5th August. The lowest reading of the thermometer was —43.0 on the 4th February.

The total depth of rain that fell during the year was 22.955 inches ; the total depth of snow was 74.21 ; total depth of rain and melted snow, 29.184 inches.

The number of rainy days, 61 ; total number of snowy days, 40.

The highest wind in the year was from 6 p.m. to 6.15 p.m. on the 13th December ; average, 40 miles per hour.

The most windy day in the year was the 1st June : average, 22.92 miles per hour.

The least windy day in the year was the 12th March ; average, 0.33 miles per hour.

April 9th, wild geese seen.
April 10th, robins seen.
April 19th, frogs seen.
April 21st, ice began to move on the Red River.
April 24th, Red River open.
April 25th, arrival of the first steamboat.
April 26th, musquitoes seen and felt.
June 27th, heavy hailstorm at 4 p.m.
August 31st, lunar rainbow in the north-west at 8.30 p.m.
November 13th, Red River frozen over.
December 13th, heavy storm from north-west, broke out at 4 p.m. ; the air was filled with drifting snow ; many persons travelling lost their way ; several deaths happened from freezing, and many were badly injured.

GENERAL METEOROLOGICAL MEANS AND PHENOMENA,

For the last Five Years, at Winnipeg, Manitoba.

By JAMES STEWART, Signal Observer.

PHENOMENA.	1872	1873	1874	1875	1876
Mean yearly temperature	32.84	32.29	32.88	29.63	31.34
Highest temperature	99.5	94.3	94.5	94.3	95.0
Lowest temperature	—41.0	—36.0	—38.7	—41.6	—43.0
Mean barometric pressure	29.1125	29.1295	29.1451	29.1474	29.3391
Mean elasticity of aqueous vapour	.208	.217	.222	.219	.230
Mean humidity of the air	71	82	82	84	94
Total amount of rain, in inches	21.62	13.58	14.99	12.29	22.96
Total amount of snow "	61.61	36.85	36.17	47.11	74.21
Total amount of rain and melted snow	30.17	17.04	18.32	16.85	29.18
Red River cleared of ice	May 2nd	April 26th	April 30th	April 29th	April 24th
Red River frozen over	Nov. 12th	Oct. 28th	Nov. 11th	Nov. 4th	Nov. 13th

The grasshoppers first appeared in this country in the year 1818, six years after the commencement of the Red River settlement.

They did not do much harm in that year, but in 1819 they destroyed the crops, and for three successive years the hopes of the husbandman. They did not, however, appear again for thirty-six years until 1864, but did no great harm till 1868, when they swept the entire crop of the settlement. We cannot deny that this country has been severely scourged by these pests, of late years; but it is the opinion of many of the oldest settlers that we will not be again visited by them to any great extent for a period of years, and by that time, the advance of settlements will have a tendency to restrict their ravages.

It is not our desire to hide defects, and while we admit the grasshoppers to be a great scourge, at the same time their visits are only occasional, and there is every reason to believe, that since they have visited this country so much of late years, we will be freed from their ravages for some time. One fact is worthy of mention, that a total destruction of crops has only taken place six times within fifty-nine years, which, it must be admitted, is a small average, and not sufficient to deter any one from settling in the country on that account. Honourable Mr. Sutherland, in his testimony before a Select Committee of the House of Commons at Ottawa, gives the following statement on the 3rd of April, 1876 :—

"I think (he says) that extensive settlement will prevent the ravages of the grasshoppers, and we have good reason to believe that we will be exempt from them during the coming season, as there were no deposits of eggs in the Province last year (a prediction verified by fact afterwards, as there were no grasshoppers last summer), and in all probability we will be relieved from that plague for many years to come. To my own knowledge, the Province was not affected by grasshoppers for twenty years previous to 1867, since which date we have had them off and on about every two years, or each alternate year."

The fall of snow on the prairie is on an average from twenty to twenty-four inches, and as there are no thaws in the winter, it does not pack, but is dry and light and disappears very quickly, allowing the husbandman to commence his labours at an early date.

The fences used in the country consist of posts and poles of spruce and poplar, the latter of which, with the bark removed, will last twenty years. Fences made of pine or basswood are sometimes used, but they are more expensive, and no better than those of spruce and poplar.

Poplar and oak wood are chiefly used as fuel, and there is not likely to be ever a scarcity of the former, as it is reproduced very rapidly.

Referring to the description of wood in Manitoba, S. J. Dawson, Esq., in his report to the Government, remarks as follows :

"The prevailing growth everywhere is poplar, and how this species of wood should be so prevalent on soil so different from what it grows on in Canada, is due to the fires which so frequently sweep over the country. A prairie or forest even over which the fire has passed, is just ready to receive the downy seeds of the poplar, which in the month of June are constantly floating in the air. The Indians say, and I think there can be no doubt of the fact, that but for the fires the prairies would soon be overgrown with wood. Be this as it may, the rapidity of the growth of the poplar, once it has taken root in the rich soil of these plains, is truly astonishing."

As a means of precaution, and as an encouragement to settlers to cultivate the growth of wood, the Government have inserted the following clause in the Dominion Lands' Act in reference to forest tree culture :—

FOREST TREE CULTURE.

Any person, male or female, being a subject of Her Majesty by birth or naturalization, and having attained the age of eighteen years, shall be entered for one quarter section or less quantity of unappropriated Dominion lands, as a claim for forest tree planting.

Application for such entry shall be made (Form F.) for the purpose of cultivating forest trees thereon, and the applicant shall make an affidavit (Form G.) that he or she is over eighteen years of age; that he or she has not previously obtained an entry of land for forest tree culture, the extent of which, added to that now applied for, will exceed in all one hundred and sixty acres; that the land is open prairie and without timber, and is unoccupied and unclaimed, and belongs to the class open for entry for tree culture; and that the application is made for his or her exclusive use and benefit.

The applicant shall pay at the time of applying, an office fee of ten dollars, for which he or she shall receive a receipt and also a certificate of entry, and shall thereon be entitled to enter into possession of the land.

No patent shall issue for the land so entered until the expiration of six years from the date of entering into possession thereof, and any assignment of such land shall be null and void unless permission to make the same shall have been previously obtained from the Minister of the Interior.

At the expiration of six years the person who obtained the entry, or if not living, his or her legal representative or assigns shall receive a patent for the land so entered, on proof to the satisfaction of the Local Agent as follows :—

1. That eight acres of the land entered had been broken and prepared for tree planting within one year after entry, an equal

quantity during the second year, and sixteen additional acres within the third year after such date.

2. That eight acres of the land entered had been planted with forest trees during the second year, an equal quantity during the third year, and sixteen additional acres within four years of the date of entry, the trees so planted being not less than twelve feet apart each way.

3. That the above area—that is to say, one fifth of the land—has for the last two years of the term been planted with timber, and that the latter has been regularly and well cultivated and protected from the time of planting : provided that in cases where the land entered is less in extent than one quarter section or one hundred and sixty acres, then the respective areas required to be broken and planted under this and the two next preceding sub-sections shall be proportionately less in extent.

If at any time within the period of six years as above, the claimant fails to do the breaking up or planting, or either, as required by this Act or any part thereof, or fails to cultivate, protect and keep in good condition such timber, then and upon such event the land entered shall be liable to forfeiture in the discretion of the Minister of the Interior, and may be dealt with in the same manner as Homesteads which may have been cancelled for non-compliance with the law.

Provided that no person who may have obtained pre-emption entry of a quarter section of land in addition to his Homestead entry under the provisions of sub-section one of section thirty-three of the said "Dominion Lands Acts," as amended by the Act of 1874 and by this Act, shall have the right to enter a third quarter section as a tree planting claim ; but such person, if resident upon his Homestead, may have the option of changing the pre-emption entry of the quarter-section or a less quantity of such quarter section for one under the foregoing provisions, and on fulfilling the preliminary conditions as to affidavit and fee, may receive a certificate for such quarter section or for such portion thereof as may have been embraced in the application, and thereupon the land included in such change of entry shall become subject in all respects to the provisions of this Act relating to tree planting.

Any person who may have been entered for a tree planting claim under the foregoing provisions, and whose right may not have been forfeited for non-compliance with the provisions thereof, shall have the same rights of possession, and to eject trespassers from the land entered by him, as are given to persons on homesteads ; and the title to land entered for a tree planting claim shall remain in the Government until the issue of a patent therefor, and such land shall not be liable to be taken in execution before the issue of the patent.

TO MANITOBA AND THE NORTH-WEST. 51

The causes of prairie fires are numerous—Indians probably most frequently set fire to them in order the more easily to find out their game. Haymakers do the same for the sake of clearing the ground of old grass, and camp fires and numerous smokers do the rest. These fires happen only in the spring and fall in old grass, and it must be remembered they only occur on the open prairie. Crops are seldom, if ever, injured by them, and where fields are cultivated and fenced, the fires do not reach. Settlers when making hay, however, if they build their stacks out in the prairie, should plough several furrows round them, so as to stop the flames from reaching them. It is always better, however, to remove the hay when made as soon as possible to your farm yard, so as to make sure of your crop and prevent any possibility of its destruction by fire. As the country opens up these fires will become less frequent.

The prices in Manitoba of Agricultural implements can be seen by the following list:—

Breaking Plows, $25.
Common do $18.
Reapers, $100 to $150.
Mowers, $75 to $125.
Reapers and Mowers combined, $150 to $200.
Horse Hay Rakes, $35.
Waggons, American manufacture, as good as made in Canada, $80.
Fanning Mills, $40.
Spades, $1 each.
Shovels, $1.25 each.
Hay Forks, 75 cents.
Manure Forks, $1 each.
Harrows, $15.

The prices of the following staple articles will give some idea of the cost of living in Manitoba:—

Tea per lb., 50 to 55 cents.
Sugar per lb., 10 to 12 cents.
Coffee per lb., 22 to 33 cents.
Tobacco, black, 50 cents.
  do smoking, 50 to 55 cents.
Coal Oil, per gallon, 50 cents.
Syrup, do 75 to 80 cents.
Pails, each, 3 hoop, 30 cents; 2 hoop, 25 cents.
Tubs, 16 inch, 90 cents each.
A good stout Suit of Clothing for a man, from $8 to $15.
Blankets, grey, per pair, $1.50 to $3.
Canadian Blankets, white, per lb., 55 to 75 cents.
Cotton, per yard, white, 8 to $12\frac{1}{2}$ cents; grey 8 to 12 cents.

Prints, 8 to 12 cents ; Winceys, 8 to 25 cents.
Woollen Stockings, per pair, 25 to 30 cents.
Flannel Shirts, each, 75 cents to $1 25.
Men's Boots, $2 to $3.
Women's Boots, $1.25 to $1.75.
Felt Hats, 75 cents to $1.

In household fittings the following prices are quoted for good plain articles:—

Table, $3.50 to $4.
Chair, 75 cents to $1.
Bedstead, $4 to $4.50.
Bureau, $8 to $12.
Kitchen Stove, No. 8, good.
Complete Furniture, $27.
Cup and Saucer, 8 to 15 cents.
Plate, 8 to 20 cents.
Coal Oil Lamp, 60 cents to $1, complete.
Axes, $1.25 to $1.50.

In Building Material :—

Good plain Lumber, $20 per M.
Good dressed Lumber, $25 to $30 per M.
Shingles, $4 to $6 per M.
Lath, $5.
Nails, 5 cents per lb., or $4 per keg.
Lime, 25 cents per bushel at the kiln.
Doors, $1.50 to $2.50 each.
Sash, 8x10, $1 per pair.
A good Single Harness, $20 to $25.
  do Double   do $35 to $40.

In the above we have only given quotations for a few of the principal articles required by a settler, so as to give you an idea of the general cost of goods in Manitoba, and we are of opinion that parties can purchase to better advantage in this Province, than to bring their old worn-out effects with them, and pay freight on them. The reason why merchants in Manitoba are able to sell so cheap is, because they purchase direct in European markets instead of through second hands.

MANITOBA MARKETS.

For many years to come an increasing home consumption will create a local demand sufficient to prevent any exportation in the way of breadstuffs of consequence. The prosecution of public works in the north-west by the Government of the Dominion, will cause a heavy demand for breadstuffs and other supplies, which the farmers of Manitoba will be in the best position to supply. So far there has been a heavy importation of flour, oats, and other farm produce from the United States into the Province, simply because we have been unable to supply the demand. It is gratifying, therefore, to the intending settler, to learn that he is sure of a ready market for his produce when he raises it, and it will be years, even allowing that we have a heavy immigration in the future, ere we will be obliged to find a market in the east for our breadstuffs. Milling facilities are on the increase throughout the Province, and farmers are therefore able to turn their wheat into flour to supply the heavy demand for that article. We can furnish a better article than can be imported from the United States, and it is reasonable to suppose that we can sell at lower prices when the cost of transportation is taken into consideration. The continual increase to our population which is going on, requires the settled farmer to supply the new arrivals with food until they can raise their own, and this is another cause of our large home demand.

The following prices for produce have ruled in Winnipeg market for some time past, meeting ready sales at the quotations named below:—

Flour (best), per 100 lbs .... $2 50 to $3 25
Wheat, per bushel 1 00
Oats,   " 0 50
Barley,   " 0 45
Butter (fresh), per lb 0 40
   "   (packed), "   .... 0 30 to 0 35
Eggs, per dozen 0 40
Pork by the hog, per lb .... 0 10 to 0 13
Beef, quarter or animal, per lb .... 0 7½ to 0 10
Potatoes, per bushel.................... 0 25 to 0 50
    Usual quotation being from 25c. to 30c., but reaching at certain seasons 50c. and as high as $1 per bushel.

The roads leading to Winnipeg from all parts of the Province are good, and farmers find no difficulty in bringing in their produce even from a distance. In fact, the travelled roads are generally of nature's make, level and hard, and even after a heavy rain, one day's sun will dry them sufficiently to enable heavily laden teams to pass over them. Every year they are improving so far as bridges and culverts are concerned, as the Local Government each summer, spends a certain sum of money building new bridges on *coulées* or streams where they are necessary, and in keeping the old ones in repair. Thus every facility, natural and mechanical, is afforded the farmer in this new country to bring his produce to market.

Just before the close of last season's navigation, an experiment was made through an enterprising house in Winnipeg, of exporting a certain quantity of Manitoba wheat for seed purposes, the order coming from Messrs. Steele Bros. & Co., of Toronto. The venture was a successful one, and will probably be followed in the future by larger shipments from this Province.

We quote the following, as showing the opinion of Ontario people as to the superiority of our grain for seed, and there is not a doubt but that Manitoba wheat will be eagerly sought for by Eastern farmers, whenever they can get it, thus opening up the way for a heavy exportation from this Province.

Before giving the quotation however, we must say that the wheat in question was grown from seed brought from Minnesota, which turned out to be a very poor sample of grain, and therefore, that which was sent to Ontario from this country, was not a fair specimen of what can be produced in Manitoba.

MANITOBA WHEAT IN ONTARIO.

The *Globe* says:—"Manitoba seed wheat will likely be largely sown in the spring by the farmers of Ontario, a considerable quantity having been imported foom the Red River Valley through the enterprise of Steele Bros. & Co., of this city. Frequent changing of seed is well known to be highly beneficial, and the excellent quality of the North-Western grain is highly favourable to its use for this purpose.

And the Belleville *Intelligencer* says:—" Hon. Robert Read has shown us a specimen of Red River spring wheat, which closely resembles the Fife wheat grown here, and may be considered a fair sample. As wheat-growing has, to use a phrase more expressive than polite, become "played out" in this section of the Dominion, it is a matter worthy of consideration whether a change of seed would not be effective in making wheat growing once more profitable to our farmers. In such case, the fine grain of the Red River country might prove of inestimable value, as the latitude and longitude of the place of its production are very different from those of the county of Hastings. We understand that a large quantity of this grain has been imported into Ontario for seed purposes."

We want, therefore, farmers to settle in the country and till the soil, so as to enable our supply to keep pace with our demand.

We also require immediate railway communication with the East, and in this connection we are happy to say the Dominion Government appear alive to this important matter. The

Canada Pacific Section, connecting Manitoba with Lake Superior, is being pushed forward as rapidly as circumstances will permit, and when it is finished we will have direct communication with the seaboard, through the chain of Lakes and the River St. Lawrence. This, in the future, will be our cheapest route of exporting our surplus grain and bringing in our supplies. In the meantime, however, we are glad to observe that an early completion of the branch road to Pembina is contemplated, so as to connect us with the American railways. The iron for this road has already been brought into the Province by the Government, and is now lying piled on the banks of the Red River, ready to be placed on the ties as soon as they are cut, and the bed of the line has been graded from Winnipeg to Pembina. The heavy cost of freighting, *via* the Red River, is a drawback to this country, and almost an obstacle to exportation; and the completion of the Pembina Road will be a great boon to the Province. There is no doubt that as soon as the railway is in running order to the boundary line, the Americans will have finished the building of their road to St. Vincent, and this will give us immediate railway communication with the outside world. In the future, the two routes—viz., the one through our own territory to Lake Superior, and the other *via* Pembina and the States—will be great competing lines for the trade of the North-West; and as their centre of competition will be Winnipeg, the importance of that city will be increased in proportion. All trunk lines require feeders, and several local roads are already contemplated for the near future, all of them being so projected as to have them terminate in Winnipeg, in order to give themselves the advantage of the competing lines eastward. Thus, like Chicago, the City of Winnipeg is bound, by the force of circumstances, to become the centre of a network of railways, all of which will assist in developing this great country and enriching the hardy people.

To the westward the Canada Pacific will open up a splendid country, vast in extent, and equal in quality to that of Manitoba; and the products of that great territory rolling into the Province for exportation to the Eastern markets, will not only add to the importance of the Province as a point of transhipment, but will assist to build up cities and towns, and raise her merchants to eminence and wealth.

The competing route to the Canada Pacific, westward, will be *via* the River Saskatchewan and Lake Winnipeg and Manitoba, and already there is a fine steamer on the former, and a staunch propeller on Lake Winnipeg, running in connection with each other, and forming a line of water communication between the Red River and Fort Edmonton. Already many tons of freight have been transhipped at Winnipeg, from the

Red River steamers to the propeller "Colville," taken by her to Grand Rapids, on Lake Winnipeg, and there transferred, by means of a short tramway of three miles, across the Portage to the steamer "Northcote," for transportation to the several places on the Saskatchewan. Thus it will be seen that Winnipeg is not only a centre of land communication but also of water.

Of the great future of the Canada Pacific, as a highway across this Continent, we can only refer our readers to the following comparison of distances by that route over the Union Pacific, of the United States:—

	To Victoria.	To San Francisco.
From Amoor	3,895	4,110
" Shanghai	5,215	5,439
" Canton	5,975	6,140
" Melbourne	6,930	7,205

The great fur trade of the North-West, in which not only the Hudson's Bay Company, but also numerous fur traders, are enengaged, the prosecution of surveys, and the building of the Canada Pacific Railway and other public works, all unite in creating for Manitoba a gigantic commerce.

The opening up of the country within the Province, and also outside its limits, is another source of trade, and when it is considered that business is only in its infancy in the North-West, the following figures will probably surprise many who have not given the matter sufficient consideration.

From the official returns of the Dominion Government for 1875, we find as follows for the Port of Winnipeg:—

Exports	$588,958 00
Imports	1,243,309 00
Entered for consumption	1,227,905 00
Duty collected	171,430 86

The increase of the carrying trade to Manitoba may be seen by the following statement of tonnage from season of 1873 by Red River steamboats:—

1873	23,613,036
1874	37,626,200
1875	76,078,680

The above figures will serve to show that the trade of Manitoba, considering that it is the youngest Province of the Dominion, is not small. The commerce of the North-West is, however, steadily on the increase, and with railway facilities it will more than double in the course of a year or two.

The branch office of the Merchants' Bank, in Winnipeg, is one of the best paying agencies of that institution, thus showing that the trade of Manitoba is worthy of cultivation ; and the Ontario Bank, lately established, is doing a good business, which is steadily on the increase.

HOMESTEAD LAW.

A liberal homestead law is in force in Manitoba, which exempts from seizure the debtor's ordinary furniture, tools and farm implements in use, also " one cow, two oxen, one horse, four sheep, two pigs and the food for the same for thirty days, and the land cultivated by the debtor, provided the extent of the same be not more than one hundred and sixty acres, in which case the surplus may be sold with privileges to first mortgagees." The house, stables, barns, fences, on the debtor's farm are by this Act declared free from seizure by virtue of all writs of execution issued by any court of this Province No limit is placed on the value of the farm or home thus secured to the family, whatever its value may become. This law may unworthily shield some, but on the other hand it will protect many worthy and honest men, women and children, and on that account is a great boon to the settler.

Thousands of acres of splendid land in the Province are at present locked up by the system of reserve, but an agitation is now going on to induce the Dominion Government to open them for settlement. There is no doubt the voice of the people will be heard, and the Government of Canada will see the wisdom of throwing open the land for cultivation. When this is done and the vexed question of Reserves settled, a large area of fine country will be placed in the market, and intending settlers will have the opportunity of securing many choice localities therefrom.

THE GOVERNMENT.

The form of government is similar to that of the other Provinces of the Dominion, but the Legislative Council was abolished by Act of the Legislature in February, 1876. The Legislature now consists only of a Legislative Assembly of twenty-four members representing twenty-four constituencies.

The Executive consists of the Lieutenant-Governor, Provincial Treasurer, Provincial Secretary and Attorney-General, Minister of Public Works and Minister of Agriculture, who is also President of the Council.

There are now the following Agricultural Societies in the Province:

The Marquette,
" Selkirk,
" Provencher,
" Lisgar,
and the Provincial.

All of which have their regular annual exhibitions to promote the interests of the husbandman, and bring this fine country into notice.

A COMPARISON.

A comparison of the yield of wheat for past years in Manitoba with the best districts of the United States, will show its superiority over them, viz:

Manitoba wheat produces 40 bushels per acre.
Minnesota,   " 20   "   "
Wisconsin,   " 14   "   "
Pennsylvania,   "   15   "   "
Massachusetts,   " 16   "   "

THE PRESENT SETTLERS.

The settlers at present in Manitoba consist of the following classes :

English half-breeds,
French half-breeds,
Scotch settlers,
Canadians from Ontario and Quebec,
Mennonites, French from Quebec and United States.

Besides these there are other nationalities, but not in sufficient numbers to distinguish them in the light of classes.

The English half-breed is generally a thrifty, careful and industrious man, retiring in disposition to such a degree that strangers are apt to consider him morose and unsocial. On the contrary, however, he is kind and hospitable, and many a settler coming into the country has had reason to thank the English half-breed for the hand of attention and fellowship extended towards him. There are, however, especially amongst the poorer people of this class, a few who from former habits of roving over the prairies and on the lakes have been unable to settle down to farming, and in consequence have not succeeded well as settlers, but they are the exceptions.

The French half breed is a light hearted individual, fonder, as a rule, of play than work. Hospitable in the extreme— when you visit his home the best he has is placed before you.

Shortly after the troubles which ushered Manitoba into Confederation there existed a strong feeling in the minds of

Canadians against the French half-breeds, but this of late years has died out, and we never see it shown, at least outwardly. There seems in fact to be a strong feeling of union at present amongst all classes whether native or otherwise, and all appear anxious to further the interests of the country generally. The French half-breeds in former years were the principal hunters and traders of the plain, and in consequence, their habits became more of a roving than a settled character, and now the work of farming is distasteful to them. They only cultivate a sufficient area of land to provide themselves with the necessaries of life, and therefore have little if any produce to dispose of. There are, however, exceptions to this rule, as some of the largest farmers and stock-raisers in the Province are French half-breeds, and the whole class, as a rule are improving as agriculturists.

The Scotch settler is a canny industrious man, careful of his means, and hoarding his pennies as others would pounds. I must not be considered, however, by this, that he is mean and parsimonious, on the contrary he is very kind in his own home when you visit him. He respects his guests, but if you are inclined to bargain with him you must be prepared to cut the matter very fine, as he will have every "bawbee" out of you that he can before he concludes with you. They are good husbandmen, and have ever exhibited a very great degree of forethought, so much so that it is proverbial in the Province that you can never find a Scotch settler in want. They do not farm extensively, but what they do they do well. The parish of Kildonan is principally settled by this class.

The Canadians are from all parts of the Dominion, and represent the usual class of farmers and mechanics in the other Provinces.

The French from the United States are those who settled in that country, but becoming discontented with it are flocking back to Canada, and are now immigrating to this Province. They declare themselves well pleased with the country and the prospects before them.

The Mennonites are a very industrious and hardy class of settlers, but so economical and saving in their habits that they spend very little money and by their hoarding propensities rather retard than advance circulation.

Educational matters in the Province are in the hands of men who give the subject an earnest attention, and although many reforms are necessary in the present system, the evils complained of will doubtless ere long be remedied. It is not our business to enter upon the merits or demerits of any system of education, it is sufficient to say that school matters in Manitoba, notwithstanding many drawbacks, are progressing well, and at a recent meeting of the Protestant School Board it was stated by the Superintendent that there were forty-three Protestant School Districts in the Province—thirty schools in operation, and 1,600 children on the various school rolls.

The total number of churches under their several denominations are:

Episcopalians	16	churches
Roman Catholics	12	"
Presbyterians	8	"
Wesleyan Methodist	7	"
Episcopal "	2	"
Baptist	2	"

The Collegiate Institutions are as follows:—St. John's College; St. Boniface College; Manitoba College; Wesleyan Institute; and there are measures being now taken to establish a University and Normal Schools for teachers.

The societies, religious, national, literary, &c. are:

Young Men's Christian Association.
St. Jean Baptiste Society.
St. Andrew's   "
St. Patrick's   "
St. George's   "
Kildonan Literary "
Winnipeg Dramatic and Literary Society.
Manitoba Colonization Society.
Manitoba Club.
Manitoba Lacrosse Club.
Selkirk Cricket Club.
St. John's College Cricket Club.
Sons of Temperance.
Independent Order of Good Templars, 2 lodges.
United Temperance Order, 3 lodges.
Odd Fellows, 3 lodges.
Masons, 7 lodges.

The following are the Post Offices in the Province:—

Winnipeg,
Baié St. Paul,
Boyne,
Burnside,
Cook's Creek,
Dynevor,
Greenwood,
Headingly,
High Bluff,
Kildonan,
Lower Fort Garry,
Loretto,

Middle Church,
Oak Land,
Oak Point,
Ossowo,
Palestine,
Parks Creek,
Peguis,
Pigeon Lake,
Poplar Point,
Portage la Prairie,
Prairie Grove,
Rockwood,

St. Agathe,	Scratching River,
St. Andrew's,	Selkirk,
St. Anne,	Springfield,
St. Boniface,	Totogon,
St. Charles,	Vital.
St. François Xavier,	West Lynne,
St. James,	Westbourne,
St. Laurent,	Woodlands,
St. Norbert,	Woodside.

There is a daily mail to and from the United States and Canada, and local mails leave the Winnipeg Post Office twice a week. There is also a mail from Winnipeg for the Saskatchewan every three weeks. Express and telegraph offices are established in Winnipeg, and connect with the eastern lines.

The City of Winnipeg is connected also with the Saskatchewan country by telegraph, and regular despatches are daily received to and from there.

ADVICE TO THE IMMIGRANT.

Having now exhausted all the practical information in regard to the Province of Manitoba which we deem necessary to the immigrant, we will proceed to give such advice as we think may be of service to those who may come to the North-West to settle or invest their means.

In the first place, the farmer who intends making his home here, ought to arrive during the spring or early summer, so as to enable him to secure his land, build a house and stables, and break some ground before the winter sets in. He may, by commencing work in the spring, succeed in obtaining a partial crop from his farm. Potatoes, for instance, may be planted as late as the beginning of June, and a fair yield realized from newly broken land. Barley and turnips also do well on the freshly turned prairie. May and June are the two best months for breaking prairie, although it can be done in July, but ought not to be attempted later in the season.

The first thing the farmer should do on his arrival is to go to the land office, and ascertain the most desirable localities open for settlement. It will not take him long then to make a personal inspection and select a place. There are several ways of obtaining land in the Province, as follows :—

HOMESTEAD RIGHTS.

All persons interested in obtaining Homestead Grants or purchasing Dominion Lands will give attention to the following provisions respecting the Public Lands of the Dominion :—

Unappropriated Dominion Lands, the surveys of which have been duly made and confirmed, shall, except as otherwise hereinafter provided, be open for purchase at the rate of one dollar per acre ; but no such purchase of more than a section, or six hundred and forty acres, shall be made by the same person : provided that whenever so ordered by the Minister of the Interior, such unoccupied lands as may be deemed by him expedient from time to time, may be withdrawn from ordinary sale or settlement, and offered at public sale (of which sale due and sufficient notice will be given), at the upset price of one dollar per acre, and sold to the highest bidder.

Payment for lands purchased in the ordinary manner shall be made in cash, except in the case of payment by scrip, or in military bounty warrants, as provided by law.

Any person, male or female, who is the sole head of a family, or any male who has attained the age of eighteen years, shall be entitled to be entered for one quarter section, or a less quantity, of unappropriated Dominion Lands, for the purpose of securing a Homestead Right in respect thereof.

The entry of a person for a Homestead Right shall entitle him to receive at the same time therewith an entry for any adjoining quarter section then unclaimed, and such entry shall entitle such person to take and hold possession and cultivate such quarter section in addition to his homestead, but not to cut wood thereon for sale or barter ; and at the expiration of the period of three years, or upon the sooner obtaining a patent for the homestead, under the fifteenth sub-section of section thirty-three of "The Dominion Lands Act," shall entitle him to a pre-emption of the said adjoining quarter section at the Government price of one dollar per acre ; but the right to claim such pre-emption shall cease and be forfeited, together with all improvements on the land, upon any forfeiture of the homestead right under the Dominion Lands Act.

Provided always, that the right to a pre-emption entry as above given, shall not belong to any settler brought in under the provisions of sections fourteen and fifteen of the said Act.

When two or more persons have settled on, and seek to obtain a title to, the same land, the Homestead Right shall be in him who made the first settlement.

Every person claiming a Homestead Right on surveyed land must, previously to settlement on such land, be duly entered therefor with the local agent within whose district such land may be situate ; but in the case of a claim from actual settlement in then unsurveyed lands, the claimant must file such application within three months after due notice has been received at the local office of such land having been surveyed, and the survey thereof confirmed ; and proof of settlement and improvement shall be made to the local agent at the time of filing such application.

A person applying for leave to be entered for lands with a view of securing a Homestead Right thereon, must make affidavit before the local agent (form B.), that he is over eighteen years of age, that he has not previously obtained a homestead under the provisions of the Dominion Lands Act; that the land in question belongs to the class open for homestead entry ; that there is no person residing or having improvements thereon ; and that his application is made for his exclusive use and benefit, and with the intention to reside upon and cultivate the said lands.

Upon making this affidavit and filing it with the local agent (and on payment to him of an office fee of *ten dollars*—for which he shall receive a receipt from the agent), he shall be permitted to enter the land specified in the application.

No patent shall be granted for the land until the expiration of *three years* from the time of entering into possession of it, except as hereinafter provided.

At the expiration of three years, the settler or his widow, her heirs or devisees—or if the settler leaves no widow, his heirs or devisees—upon proof to the satisfaction of the local agent that he or his widow, or his or her representatives as aforesaid, or some of them, have (except in the case of entry upon contiguous lands as hereinbefore provided), resided upon and cultivated the land for the three years next after the filing of the affidavit for entry, or in the case of a settler on unsurveyed land, who may upon the same being surveyed, have filed his application as provided in sub-section five, upon proof, as aforesaid, that he or his widow, or his or their representatives, as aforesaid, or some of them, have resided upon and cultivated the land for the three years next preceding the application for patent, shall be entitled to patent for the land, provided such claimant is then a subject of Her Majesty by birth or naturalization.

Provided always, that the right of the claimant to obtain a patent under the said sub-section as amended, shall be subject to the provisions of section fifteen herein lastly quoted.

Provided further, that in case of settlements being formed of immigrants in communities (such, for instance, as those of Mennonites or Icelanders), the Minister of the Interior may vary or waive, in his discretion, the foregoing requirements as to residence and cultivation on each separate quarter-section entered as a homestead.

When both parents die without having devised the land, leaving a child or children under age, it shall be lawful for the executors (if any), of the last surviving parent, or the guardian or guardians of such child or children, with the approval of a

Judge of a Superior Court of the Province or Territory in which the lands lie, to sell the lands for the benefit of the infant or infants, but for no other purpose ; and the purchaser in such case shall receive a patent for the lands so purchased.

The title to lands shall remain in the Crown until the issue of the patent therefor ; and such lands shall not be liable to be taken in execution before the issue of the patent.

In case it is proved to the satisfaction of the Minister of the Interior that the settler has voluntarily relinquished his claim, or has been absent from the land entered by him for more than *six months* in any one year without leave of absence from the Minister of the Interior, then the right to such land shall be liable to forfeiture, and may be cancelled by the said Minister ; and the settler so relinquishing or abandoning his claim shall not be permitted to make more than a second entry.

Any person who has availed himself of the foregoing provisions may, before the expiration of three years, obtain a patent for the land entered upon by him, including the wood lot, if any, appertaining to the same, as hereinafter provided, on paying the Government price thereof at the date of entry, and making proof of settlement and cultivation for not less than twelve months from the date of entry.

Proof of actual settlement and cultivation shall be made by affidavit of the claimant before the local agent, corroborated on oath by two credible witnesses.

The Minister of the Interior may at any time order an inspection of any homestead or homesteads in reference to which there may be reason to believe the foregoing provisions, as regards settlement and cultivation, have not been, or are not being carried out, and may, on a report of the facts, cancel the entry of such homestead or homesteads ; and in the case of a cancelled homestead, with or without improvements thereon, the same shall not be considered as of right open for fresh entry, but may be held for sale of the land and of the improvements, or of the improvements thereon, in connection with a fresh homestead entry thereof, at the discretion of the Minister of the Interior.

All assignments and transfers of Homestead Rights before the issue of the patent shall be null and void, but shall be deemed evidence of abandonment of the right ; and the person so assigning or transferring shall not be permitted to make a second entry.

Any person who may have obtained a Homestead entry shall be considered, unless and until such entry be cancelled, as having an exclusive right to the land so entered as against any other person or persons whomsoever, and may bring and maintain action for trespass committed on the said land, or any part thereof.

The provisions relating to Homesteads shall only apply to agricultural lands ; that is to say, they shall not be held to apply to lands set apart as timber limits or as hay lands, or to lands valuable for stone or marble quarries, or those having water-power thereon which may be useful for driving machinery.

Any Homestead claimant who, previous to the issue of the patent, shall sell any of the timber on his claim, or on the wood lot appertaining to his claim, to saw-mill proprietors, or to any other than settlers for their own private use, shall be guilty of trespass, and may be prosecuted therefor before a Justice of the Peace ; and upon conviction thereof shall be subject to a fine or imprisonment, or both ; and further, such person shall forfeit his claim absolutely.

If any person or persons undertake to settle any of the public lands of the Dominion free of expense to the Government, in the proportion of one family to each alternate quarter section, or not less than sixty-four families in any one township, under the Homestead provisions of the Act hereby amended, the Governor in Council may withdraw any such township from public sale and general settlement, and may, if he thinks proper, having reference to the settlement so affected, and to the expense incurred by such person or persons in procuring the same, order the sale of any other and additional lands in such township to such person or persons, at a reduced price, and may make all necessary conditions and agreements for carrying the same into effect.

The expenses, or any part thereof, incurred by any person or persons, for the passage money or subsistence in bringing out an immigrant, or for aid in erecting buildings on the Homestead, or in providing farm implements or seed for such immigrants, may, if so agreed upon by the parties, be made a charge on the Homestead of such immigrant ; and in case of such immigrant attempting to evade such liability by obtaining a Homestead entry outside of the land withdrawn under the provisions of the next preceding section, then and in such case the expense incurred on behalf of such immigrant as above, shall become a charge on the Homestead so entered, which, with interest thereon, must be satisfied before a patent shall issue for the land ; provided as follows :—

(a) That the sum or sums charged for the passage money and subsistence of such immigrant shall not be in excess of the actual cost of the same, as proved to the satisfaction of the Minister of the Interior ;

(b) That an acknowledgment by such immigrant of the debt so incurred shall have been filed in the Dominion Lands office ;

(c) That in no case shall the charge for principal moneys advanced against such Homestead exceed in amount the sum of two hundred dollars ;

(*d*) That no greater rate of interest than six per cent. per annum shall be charged on the debt so incurred by such immigrant.

Then an immigrant with means can often purchase lands within the existing settlements, improved and unimproved, on advantageous terms, from the earlier settlers, who, in many instances contemplate moving further westward to take advantage of the hunting and trading on the prairie, and a farmer having some capital would often prefer to settle near churches, schools, post office, &c., &c. The land list published in January, 1876, by A. W. Burrows, General Land Agent, Winnipeg, is a proof of what we say, as in it farms in the neighbourhood of Winnipeg, Portage la Prairie, Emerson, Stoney Mountain, and other good localities, are offered at from $2 to $7 per acre.

Half-Breed Scrip, payable to bearer in 160 acres of Dominion lands, can be bought at about 50 cents per acre, or less, and are extensively used by incoming settlers for location of Government lands.

The Half-Breed Reserves, 1,400,000 acres, immediately surrounding the capital of the Province, and the old settlements on the Assiniboine River, which are now in process of distribution to the children of Half-Breeds, in parcels of 240 acres, will change hands largely at reasonable prices, and rapidly becoming settled, will hereafter teem with prosperous cultivation.

Without going into particulars, we may mention the following localities of surveyed lands which are now open for settlement :—

DOMINION LANDS NOTICE.

Notice is hereby given that, on and after the 1st day of June, 1874, the Dominion Lands in Manitoba and the North-West Territories will, until further notice, be divided into the following Land Districts, viz :

District No. 1, in charge of Head Office at Winnipeg, will comprise all lands open for sale and settlement, North of the Township line between Townships 7 and 8, and East of Lake Manitoba, and the Range line between Ranges 5 and 6, together with the settlement belt, and all lands claimed under the provisions of the 31st and 32nd clauses of the "Manitoba Act."

District No. 2, with its office at Emerson, will comprise all lands open for sale and settlement South of the Township line between Townships 7 and 8, and the International Boundary.

District No. 3, with its office at Westbourne, will comprise all lands open for sale and settlement North of the Township line between Townships 7 and 8, and West of Lake Manitoba and the Range line between Ranges 5 and 6.

All applications to purchase or Homestead Dominion Lands must be made to the officer in charge of the District within which the lands applied for are situated.

DONALD CODD,
Agent of Dominion Lands.

Dominion Lands Office,
Winnipeg, May 1st, 1874.

District No. 1.—There is very little land open for settlement in this district, as the best locations have been already claimed. You can obtain good land, however, by purchase of half-breed rights and settlers' claims.

District No. 2.—There are the greater portion of ninety-five townships open for settlement, and some of the finest land in the Province is included in them, especially that in the direction of the Pembina Mountains.

District No. 3.—There are the greater portion of 154 townships still open for settlement, and the land in the neighbourhood and westward of Palestine is splendid rolling prairie, with wood, water and hay in plenty.

Who will say, therefore, that there is no land within the limits of Manitoba or in its immediate neighbourhood open for settlement, and what inducement can there be for the immigrant to pass thousands of acres of fine country, with all the requisites for farming, and adjoining established settlements, to go away beyond them, where, perhaps, he and his family will have to undergo for years all the hardships and inconveniences of a pioneer life? We advise immigrants to locate, if not within Manitoba, at least as near its limits as possible, and, in addition, would reiterate what we have already said, that there is plenty of fine land to be obtained in the Province, and no necessity for going beyond it.

Should a settler, however, wish to take up a claim on unsurveyed land outside the Province, his plan is to locate, and commence making improvements wherever he may find a desirable spot.

If he should be unable to select a spot suited to his ideas within the limits of the Province, we would advise him to go westward beyond Palestine, and take up a claim as near the settlement as he can find one to please him. To do this he will require to act as follows. He may settle wherever he finds a place to suit him, and the Government has provided for his case as follows:—

"Any land over and above the amount allowed to a settler under the Homestead Law, he will have to pay for at the Government price of $1 per acre up to 640 acres."

Every person claiming a Homestead Right on surveyed land must, previous to settlement on such land, be duly entered therefor with the Local Agent within whose district such land may be situate, but in case of a claim from actual settlement in then unsurveyed lands, the claimant must file such application within three months after due notice shall have been received at the local office of such land having been surveyed, and the survey thereof confirmed, and proof of settlement and improvement shall be made to the local agent at the time of filing such application.

Any person can purchase by scrip any quantity of unoccupied land, surveyed or unsurveyed.

The Government has, in the Dominion Lands Act, provided as follows for the purchase of land, and for grazing, hay and wood :—

ORDINARY PURCHASE AND SALE OF LANDS.

Unappropriated Dominion lands, the surveys of which may have been duly made and confirmed, shall, except as otherwise hereinafter provided, be open for purchase at the rate of one dollar per acre ; but no such purchase of more than a section, or six hundred and forty acres, shall be made by the same person ; provided, that whenever so ordered by the Minister of the Interior, such unoccupied lands as may be deemed by him expedient from time to time may be withdrawn from ordinary sale or settlement and offered at public sale (of which sale due and sufficient notice shall be given), at the upset price of one dollar per acre, and sold to the highest bidder.

PAYMENT FOR LANDS.

Payments for lands, purchased in the ordinary manner, shall be made in cash, except in the case of payment by scrip or in military bounty warrants as hereinbefore provided.

GRAZING LANDS.

The Governor in Council may, from time to time, grant leases of unoccupied Dominion Lands for grazing purposes to any person or persons whomsoever for such term of years and at such rent in each case as may be deemed expedient ; but every such lease shall, among other things, contain a condition by which, if it should thereafter be thought expedient by the Minister of Interior to offer the land covered thereby for settlement, the said Minister may, on giving the lessee two years notice, cancel the lease at any time during the term.

HAY LANDS.

Leases of unoccupied Dominion lands, not exceeding in any case a legal sub-division of forty acres, may be granted for the purpose of cutting hay thereon, to any person or persons whomsoever, being *bona fide* settlers in the vicinity of such hay lands, for such term and at such rent fixed by public auction or otherwise as the Minister of the Interior may deem expedient; but such lease, except as may be otherwise specially agreed upon, shall not operate to prevent, at any time during the term thereof, the sale or settlement of the lands described therein under the provisions of this Act, the lessee being paid in such case by the purchaser or settler, for fencing or other improvements made on such land, such sum as shall be fixed by the Local Agent, and allowed to remove any hay he may have made.

The Minister of the Interior may direct that, in the subdivision of townships which may consist partly of prairie and partly of timber land, such of the sections or subdivisions of sections containing islands, belts, or other tracts of timber, shall be subdivided into such number of wood lots of not less than ten, and not more than twenty acres in each lot, as will afford, so far as the extent of wood land in the township may permit, one such wood lot to each quarter-section prairie farm in such township:

Provided, that neither the sections and parts of sections in each township vested in the Hudson's Bay Company by this Act, nor those sections set apart herein for schools, shall be subject in any way to the operation of the next preceding sub-clause:

3. The division of such wood lots shall be by squared posts, numbered from one upwards, marked with a marking iron, and planted in the section line bounding the timber tract so laid out; and each wood lot shall front on a section road allowance.

Provided, that in case an island or belt of timber be found in the survey of any township to lie in a quarter-section or several quarter-sections, but in such manner that no single quarter-section shall have more of such timber than twenty-five acres, such timber shall be taken to be appurtenant to such quarter-section or quarter-sections, and shall not be further divided into wood lots:

5. The Local Agent, as settlers shall apply for Homestead Rights in the township, and in the same order as such applications shall be made, shall, if so requested, apportion to each quarter-section so applied for, one of the adjacent wood lots, and such wood lot shall be paid for by the applicant at the rate of one dollar per acre, and shall be entered on the Local Agent's books and be returned by him as in connection with the home-

stead so entered; and on such homestead claimant fulfilling all the requirements of this Act in that behalf, but not otherwise, a patent shall issue to him for such wood lot:

6. Provided, that any homestead claimant, who, previous to the issue of the patent shall sell any of the timber on his claim, or on the wood lot appertaining to his claim, to saw mill proprietors or to any other than settlers for their own private use, shall be guilty of a trespass, and may be prosecuted therefor before a Justice of the Peace, and upon conviction thereof, shall be subject to a fine or imprisonment, or both; and further such person shall forfeit his claim absolutely.

It is our opinion that an immigrant would be unwise to go far beyond the line of settlement, or to undertake to go to the Saskatchewan in advance of civilization, for the following reasons:

1. The heavy cost of getting to his claim.
2. His isolation until settlements reach him.
3. The high cost for procuring the necessaries of life.
4. The distance from a market; even with the chance of selling his produce to traders and others, his profits would be eaten up by the cost of procuring necessaries which he is unable to raise on his farm.
5. His isolation from churches and schools.
6. The nearer he keeps to the line of settlement the quicker will he obtain all the benefits of civilization, especially as the march of development is rapid in this country.

It is for this reason that we condemn the idea of inducing immigrants to go to the North-West in advance of settlements, and before proper means of communication are opened up to that vast country.

It must not be understood, however, that we have any desire to belittle the Saskatchewan country, on the contrary we are of opinion that in the near future that great territory will afford homes for thousands of hardy and industrious farmers; and we are also aware that as far as climate, soil, and other advantages are concerned, the Saskatchewan is equal to Manitoba. But our desire is not to mislead people for the mere purpose of advancing immigration, and the development of the country will be sufficiently promoted by allowing the progress of settlements to be gradual rather than scattered in its character.

The Province of Manitoba although young, possesses most of the elements of civilization, and it is the centre for these to extend from and spread throughout the entire north-west. By adopting this plan of immigrants locating as near the centre of civilization as possible, our settlements will be more compact, and the new settlers will feel more contented and happy when not too far removed from comforts to which they were accustomed in the countries from which they came.

We have already given the prices of articles in Manitoba, and it is for the intending settler to decide whether to bring his household effects and farming implements with him, or purchase a new outfit on his arrival here. He will be able to judge better when he ascertains from the transportation companies, the cost of bringing old articles to this country, whether it will be better to sell them and purchase new ones in Manitoba.

The settler having made good use of the summer months, will find himself in the fall, possessed of a house, stables, and a supply of hay for his cattle, besides which he may have realized a small crop from his farm. When winter comes, he will find employment in cutting and turning fence rails to enclose his fields in the spring. He will have firewood to cut, and may collect the timber for a better house, and more stabling accommodation to be erected the succeeding summer. If the settler arrives in early spring or summer, it will be better for him to bring his family with him. The females can be of great service to him in many ways, and the young men or boys can assist him in the field and in the erection of his buildings. If they come overland from Moorhead, it will be better to continue to camp instead of going to a hotel, not only as a matter of expense, but also of health, as a frequent change from camp to house, and from house to camp, is not beneficial to health.

If the settler should find it impossible to arrive here before the fall, his best plan is to come alone without his family, and to simply decide upon a location, and if practicable, erect a house thereon. This done, he is in a position to receive his family early the next spring, but if he is obliged to bring his folks with him in the fall, let him attend without delay to the building of a house, and procuring hay for his cattle, which can be done even thus late in the season if care is taken. The winter can then be employed as usual, in getting out fence rails &c., and the breaking of land will have to remain till the spring.

The rapid development of the country and the establishment of towns and villages will for years to come cause a demand for mechanical labour and skill. This can be easily seen, and therefore mechanics of all kinds are sure to meet with employment at remunerative wages. The manufacturing interests of the country are only in their infancy and must rapidly become developed, it is not too much therefore to say that the demand for mechanical labour must increase, and a good opening presents itself to artizans of every description. Wages at present are good and must remain so while the demand for labour exists.

We will now conclude with a few remarks in regard to the future prospects of the North-West, and the country immediately outside the limits of the Province. It cannot be denied that the lands within the confines of Manitoba are being rapidly taken up, and although for many years to come there will be opportunities to procure suitable locations within the Province, the extension of the boundaries of Manitoba is only a question of a short time, and those who settle near the present limits will soon find themselves within the Province.

The country to the westward of Palestine and Beautiful Plains is one continuous prairie, with bluffs and creeks lined with wood. The land is excellent, and the settler is not obliged to go as far as the Saskatchewan to find a new home for his family. There is abundance of land of the very best description, with plenty of wa.., wood, and hay, to be found nearer home. So, settler, keep as near a market for your produce as you possibly can. When the Canada Pacific Railway is built through to the Saskatchewan country, affording communication with that vast territory, it will be time enough for immigrants to pour in, but until then let each man coming to the country with his family keep as near the line of existing settlements as he possibly can.

It appears to us unnecessary to speak of the future of this great country—the tale is told in a few words.

A vast territory which cannot be surpassed in the world for agricultural purposes; abundance of wood, water and hay, for the farmer, and a liberal policy to enable settlers to take up land; railways in progress, and others projected to intersect the entire country, and carry the products to eastern markets.

Where there is a fine agricultural country, the merchant must succeed, and when it is considered that the vast territory of unoccupied land in the United States has been proved to be little better than barren waste, it is not difficult to see that the tide of emigration from the older portions of the world must flow towards the north-west, and as the country thus rapidly fills with population, its commerce must extend and expand in proportion.

In reference to what we have stated in regard to the United States, we will conclude by quoting the words of Professor Henry, of the Smithsonian Institute, Washington.

He says: "we have stated that the entire region, west of the 98th degree of west longitude, with the exception of a small portion of western Texas, and the main border along the Pacific, is a country of comparatively little value to the agriculturist; and perhaps it will astonish the reader if we direct his attention to the fact that this line, that passes southward from Lake Winnipeg to the Gulf of Mexico, will divide the *whole surface of the United States into two nearly equal parts*. This statement, when fully appreciated, will serve to dissipate some of the dreams, which have been considered realities *as to the destiny* of the western part of the North American continent. Truth, however, transcends even the laudable feelings of pride and country, and in order properly to direct the policy of this great confederacy " (the United States), " it is necessary to be well acquainted with the theatre in which its future history is to be re-enacted."

Now, looking upon that picture and on this, let us draw the comparison. Upon the northern edge of that great Sahara, we have the valleys of the Red River and Saskatchewan, carrying their rich and grassy undulations to the gorges of the Rocky mountains; forming an isolated belt of verdure across the western half of the British American continent, an isthmus of fertile and habitable lands between the Arctic wastes, which extend to the frozen ocean on the north, and the vast deserts between the Mississippi River and the Pacific coast.

EXTRACTS FROM LOCAL PAPERS

AND CORRESPONDENCE,

To prove the correctness of the Pamphlet.

THE SOIL.

Bludgett (an American authority) states that " the basin of the Winnipeg is the seat of the greatest average wheat product on this continent, and probably *in the world*. The limestone substrata of this region, and its rich, deep, and calcareous loam on retentive clay subsoil, is always associated with a rich wheat development, while its hot and humid summers fulfil all the climatological conditions of a first-rate wheat country. Some fields on the Red River have been known to produce twenty successive crops of wheat without fallow or manure, and the yield has frequently reached as high as forty bushels per acre. An important feature in the soil of Manitoba and the North-West is, that its earthy materials are minutely pulverized, and the soil is everywhere light, mellow and spongy. With these uniform characteristics, the soils are of different grades or fertility, according to local situations. A general ingredient of the soil is sand, of which silica is the base, as of all good soils. It plays an important part in the economy of growth, and is an essential constituent in the organism of all cereals. We are told that about sixty-seven per cent. of the ash of the stems of wheat, corn, rye, barley, oats, etc., is pure silica, or flint. It is this which gives the glazed coating to the plants, and gives strength to the stalk." Now, this silica is an acid and is insoluble, but readily combines with lime, soda, magnesia, potash, and the other ingredients of our soil, and in this condition is readily available to the use of the plant, and forms an essential element' to the growth of the cereals ; from this and other causes is attributable the superiority of our wheat over all other grown east or south.

The packages of Manitoba earth are on exhibition at Ottawa, and experts there say that the soil cannot be rivalled by any other spot on earth. The specimens were taken from the Little Saskatchewan, and between the Portage and Winnipeg.

THE CLIMATE.

The first cricket match played in British North America this year came off Monday afternoon in this city. Sides were chosen by the Mayor and Mr. Richards. Although there has been very little time for practice, some excellent play was shown, some of the cricketers showing up in good form. The other side won the match.—*17th April,* 1876.

The difference :—New England States, the heaviest snow storm of the season ; Manitoba—most enjoyable weather. Comparisons are always odious.— *8th April,* 1876.

Ontario papers are filled with items about the heated term. How we can sit down and enjoy the cool breezes that waft over the Prairie Province, and pity our sweltering brothers down east.—*July 9th,* 1876.

Look at this picture :

" If several inches of snow, temperature below zero, and a blinding snow-drift constitute winter, then the genuine article has come. Saturday night and all Sunday it snowed, and the Ice King ruled in all his terror. The weather since has gradually relaxed, and nature smiles in sunshine, while the roads yawn in coagulated mud."—Sherbrooke, Quebec, *Gazette, October 20th.*

And on this :

The weather in Manitoba at the same date was cloudy, but had been fair the previous week, and glorious Indian summer prevailed.

The extreme cold weather said to prevail in Manitoba does not prevent the work of grading on the Canada Pacific Railway being carried on. And the question arises—could similar work be done in any other Province of the Dominion in the winter season ?

When our little snow storm of the 4th ult. came upon us, nearly every person expected winter at once, and as scarcely any of our settlers had their potatoes and other vegetables up, all were in a state of anxiety so long as the snow remained. The fine weather which set in immediately after its disappearance, and continues up to the present, has given ample time for getting the root crop safely stored, as well as for getting the outbuildings in shape for winter. Considerable ploughing is being done.

Mr. D. Porteous has been threshing, and his grain is turning out well. From four acres of barley he threshed 280 bushels, or 70 bushels per acre. Threshing has not, generally speaking, commenced.—*October 30th*, 1876.

A gentleman who left Ontario in the midst of a snow storm was astonished to find on his arrival here that Manitoba was enjoying perfect Florida weather. He thinks that "Hyperborean" is more applicable to other places than the Prairie Province.—*October 21st*, 1876.

First flowers found on the Prairie, April 16th.
First ploughing, April 17th.
First wild fowl seen, April 6th.

MANITOBA WHEAT.

Some Wheat.—Messrs. John R. McMillan, and John Williams, of Rockwood, have raised a quantity of wheat which weighs sixty-six pounds to the bushel. Forty-six bushels were taken to Pritchard's Mill, St. Paul's, and each sixty pounds of wheat gave the following returns:—42½ lbs. flour, 1½ lbs. middlings, 2½ lbs. coarse shorts, 8½ lbs. bran, 2 lbs. allowed for dust and dirt, and passing through the smut machine, stones, and bolts. The flour, we were told, compares with any other manufactured either inside or outside the Province. The wheat was raised on new land, and was the first crop the land produced. This exhibit was an excellent one, and any one who fancies he can beat it is requested to send on his figures.

"We have been shown some fine samples of wheat grown by Mr. Basler, at Little Saskatchewan. The wheat, which averages forty bushels to the acre, weighs sixty-eight pounds to the bushel. Mr. B. came to this country with Mr. Ralston in 1874, possessed of scarcely any of this world's goods, but now, notwithstanding the terrible ordeal through which the country has gone, is in comparatively easy circumstances, having this year five acres each in wheat, barley, oats, and potatoes, from which he secured splendid crops. He also now owns a good house, ten head of cattle, and pigs, poultry, etc."

"Fine Wheat.—An extraordinary fine sample of wheat grown by Adam McKenzie, of Beautiful Plains, has been shown us by Robt. Rolston. The wheat, of which two thousand bushels were raised, is hard, plump, and bright; and is said to have averaged from 66 to 68 lbs. per bushel. Some taken to C. P. Brown's mill, Palestine, produced 46 lbs. of flour to the bushel."

"Another Sample of Fine Wheat.—A sample of the

finest looking spring wheat we think we ever saw, has been handed us, raised by Mr. Joseph W. Johnston, of the Boyne. From a bushel and a half's sowing, forty bushels were harvested. The kernels are large, and the skin is very light in colour and thin. It weighs sixty-four pounds to the bushel. We do not know the name of the variety."

"AN extraordinary yield is shown by the following : Seventy bushels of wheat were threshed from a field where two bushels of seed were sown. The happy agriculturist is our old friend Tom Taylor, of Mapleton."

MANITOBA OATS.

"OATS.—Mr. Thos. West has on exhibition the product of one oat grain, a stool of 92 stems. On one of the stems he counted 121 grains of oats. He has a number of other very prolific stools, grown in his garden in the north ward."

"OATS.—Mr. A. H. Murray, M.P.P., has just completed the threshing out of the first seven acres of oats threshed in the parish of St. Charles this season, the gratifying result being ninety bushels to the acre ! Next !"

"OATS.—Andrew Ness, of St. Charles, sowed two bushels of Surprise oats, and harvested one hundred from them. The ground sown was only about three-fourths of an acre."

"TWENTY acres of Mr. Sifton's two hundred acre field of oats have been threshed out, and yielded seventy-five bushels to the acre. The remainder will keep up the average."

MANITOBA BARLEY.

"CROPS.—Mr. Roderick McKenzie, an old settler of Headingly, last week threshed out the product of four bushels of barley, which yielded 120 bushels, and of ten bushels of oats, which yielded over 350 bushels "

MANITOBA ROOTS AND VEGETABLES.

"GARDEN TRUCK.—Mr. Egan, of Kildonan, is doing wonders in this line, having had ripe tomatoes since the middle of August in abundance. Some roots of mangold wurtzel challenge the Province for size. A specimen shown measured three feet and a half in length and had grown two feet above ground. Send along your items and samples."

ANOTHER WHOPPER.—We were told recently of a radish grown in a garden in this city which measures 2 ft. 5¾ in. from the base of the first leaf to the tip. Next !

ROOTS AND VEGETABLES.

(*Extract from Report of Manitoba Provincial Show of* 1876.)

The display in this class is decidedly the "big thing" of

the show. The "products of Manitoba" exhibited excelled
even the expectations of the most sanguine believers in the
Prairie Province—and most certainly their huge dimensions
and unparalleled excellence could not be surpassed. Indeed,
the exhibit is so large that it is almost impossible to notice it
in detail. In quality and variety the exhibit is far beyond
that of any former year, and many visitors from Ontario pro-
nounce it to be superior to anything they ever saw—the Cen-
tennial not excepted. In potatoes the early rose was the most
numerous, but there were also some magnificent specimens of
Peerless, California, Snowflake, English, and Early Regent, and
a number of good looking varieties unnamed. There are also
several lots of seedlings of this year, but of course too small to
show any marked characteristics. It is, however, a pleasing
sign that attention is being directed to the creation of varieties
suited to the country.

Cabbages of all kinds and of immense size are exhibited.
Mr. Egan, of Kildonan, took the first prize for winter cabbage,
with a specimen that measured four feet in circumference, and
very solid. Rev. Mr. Pritchard, St. Paul's, has one that
measures fifty inches in circumference. The first prize for a
collection was awarded to John Arkland, of St. James, and
the second to William Laurie, of this city.

Turnips weighing 36 lbs. are among the monstrosities in this
line. The best specimens of white turnips were shown by Mr.
Macdonald, of Springfield, but he failed to get a prize because
he entered them under a wrong name. The varieties shown
were chiefly Swedish, yellow Aberdeen, and white.

Carrots, parsnips, mangold wurtzel, turnip and long beet,
some fine sugar beets, were in great profusion and puzzled the
judges not a little.

There were enough ripe tomatoes and melons on exhibition
to show that with care they can be raised in this country.

A number of the entries in this class were weighed, with the
results given below. The articles, it must be remembered,
were not specially selected but picked out at haphazard. The
early rose potatoes which gained the first prize averaged two
pounds each, and others of the same variety, which did not
carry off prizes, averaged but half a pound less. There were,
however, potatoes of greater weight exhibited. The 1st prize
winter drumhead cabbages weighed 25 lbs. and $23\frac{1}{2}$ lbs., and
another one balanced the scales at 23 lbs., there also being a
large number nearly reaching the same weight. The first prize
cauliflower, stripped of leaves, weighed $6\frac{1}{4}$ lbs. only; but one
to which no prize was given brought down the balance at $12\frac{1}{4}$
lbs. The latter, however, was dirty and spoiled, and was thus
debarred from gaining a prize. A $19\frac{1}{2}$ lb. mangold wurtzel
didn't even take a third prize—nor did a $36\frac{1}{2}$ lb. turnip. A

Swede weighed 21½ lbs., but also failed to carry off any honours, excepting admiration, and a white turnip 19½ lbs. The first prize beet weighed 8 lbs., and a sugar beet of the same weight carried off the third prize only. Six carrots averaged over two pounds each, and in parsnips 2¾ and 2½ lbs. specimens were plentiful. Three white onions weighed a pound apiece, and three red ones totted up 2¾ pounds—and yet these were not honoured with prize tickets. These few figures will give our readers at a distance some faint idea of the magnificence of the display in this line, in which Manitoba takes second place to none.

Melons ripen to perfection, and our garden vegetables are beyond anything I have seen in Canit' a or the Northern States. Turnip-radishes for ... reaching the enormous weight of four pounds (measu: . . inches in circumference and 9 in depth), and retaining all the go ' qualities appertaining to the smaller varieties.

Cauliflowers measuring twenty-two inches across, being by no means the exception. In proof of the earliness of our garden we, to-day, enjoyed the first salad of the season grown in the open air.—*June* 14*th*, 1876.

Mr. Sondermann, of the city, has any quantity of large tomatoes, and a Kohl-rabi as big as his head. Mr. Corbett, of Springfield, possesses a squash as big as an average-sized flour barrel.

Green corn is offered at twenty-five cents, and cabbages at thirty-five cents a dozen ; new potatoes at fifty to sixty co 's a bushel.—*August* 5*th*, 1876.

At Platt's boarding house, Selkirk, there is a beet six feet seven inches in length, of course including the tops.

Some fine ears of corn were brought into the city, Saturday, by Mr. Longbottom—the first of the season.—*August* 5*th*, 1876.

THE PROVINCIAL FAIR.

Thirty pound cabbages and turnips, 3lb. potatoes and Brobdignonian vegetables generally are so common that the marvellous show of them was only surprising to strangers.

A quantity of very fine tomatoes, which were being raised by Mr. Richard Egan, of Kildonan, for exhibition at the Provincial Agricultural Society's Show in October, were stolen the other evening from his garden.

THE MANITOBA PRODUCTS.—Mr. McLaughlin writes from Hamilton respecting his show of Manitoba products at the fair there, that the turnips, onions, red cabbage and potatoes would have taken the prize over anything exhibited. Though the grains were not a good sample, they attracted great attention. He could have sold bushels of them for seed at very high prices.

and was offered twenty-five cents each for the potatoes—no two of the early rose potatoes which took the prize there would weigh as much as any one of his would. No feature of the show attracted half as much attention as the Manitoba tent, and he was kept busy all the time explaining features of the map. Mr. McL. prophecies an unusual immigration next year.

MANITOBA POTATOES.

POTATOES.—James Sinclair, of Greenwood, gathered 262 lbs. of Snowflake potatoes from one pound planted.

Mr. Omand, of St. James, comes to the front with a five pound potato, which has been secured by Mr. Rolston, who will send it to Ontario for the people there to gaze at.

Mr. F. C. Shipp, of Point Douglas, lifted in his garden, Saturday, a potato weighing just four pounds. This was grown upon land which has been cropped for the past forty years.

Manitoba is not only to be noted for its huge potatoes but also for the enormous yield of the tubers. A quarter re patch, belonging to Mr. J. W. Sifton, of the C. P. T. y ai. ed out two hundred and seventy-five bushels—an average of eleven hundred bushels to the acre.

Recently, seventy-six potatoes were taken from one hill by Mr. Henderson, of this city, of which fifty-five were larger than hen's eggs. This is illustrative of the wonderful productiveness of this country, and shows that it is no "small potatoes, and few in a hill."

Mr. Barclay, of Stony Mountain, this season, tried potatoes on first ploughing of land, partly and thinly covered by low bush; he had doubts as to the result, as it is desirable generally to first plough the land and rot the sod prior to seeding; the result, however, was a most surprising crop under the circumstances, the return having measured 466 bushels of large healthy potatoes to the acre.

TREMENDOUS YIELD.—Mr. Mullard, of Victoria, got one pound of potatoes from Hamilton of the Early Snowflake variety, from which he has raised one hundred and sixty-one pounds. Mr. M. expects his whole potato crop to average over five hundred bushels to the acre.

Mr. F. J. Hosken has some magnificent specimens of potatoes grown in his garden at St. Boniface west, of the English Regent variety, imported from England. From one hill six huge ones, and a patent pail of smaller ones, were taken. Mr. H. intends sending samples to London, England, and show those at home what Manitoba can produce.

An Ontario paper which always thought our stories of the great size of Manitoba products were considerably larger than the vegetables, admits that its impressions were wrong, the editor having been convinced by a gentlemen whose veracity cannot be questioned, who stated that he himself had seen four pound murphies dug up from a patch here. This is only another instance of the correctness of the saying ; " Truth is mighty, and will prevail."

We were shown some remarkable potatoes from the garden of Mr. John Higgins, of the city. They are of the Early Rose varieties, and will average at least one pound each throughout the field, while numbers can be picked that weigh two and three pounds. It is also remarkable, that these potatoes are all solid, and as mealy as any murphy ever grown. Some of the hills turn up one or two tubers with respectable sized potatoes stuck all over them, each cluster being as much as the usual produce of a hill elsewhere. Mr. Higgins says that this country is the paradise for Irishmen, as it undoubtedly grows better " praties " than any other place in the world.

MANITOBA TURNIPS.

Mr. J. B. Clarke, on the Drever Farm, St. James, has seven acres in turnips—three acres of yellow Aberdeen, and four of Swedish, the product of which is beyond the average—the former about 1,200 bushels per acre, and the latter 1,000. In the absence of a lively market for this sale, Mr. C. intends feeding them to sheep and cattle.

John Taylor, Headingly, says, that he has a field of turnips of enormous size ; one turnip which he weighed turns the scales at eighteen and a half pounds.

MANITOBA GENERAL CROPS.

Mr. Winram of Sunnyside, was in town lately, and reports the crops in that township as averaging more under the thresher than was expected—wheat turning out 25 to 30 bushels, oats 75, barley 50. The former is much better in quality than anticipated, and the oats and barley are extra fine grains.

CROPS.— Mr. Gillis, of St. Andrew's, reports 195 bushels of oats, from three and a half acres of breaking ; Mr. John Fraser, of Kildonan, 70 bushels of oats per acre ; Mr. Good, of Grassmere, 37 bushels of wheat to the acre, and 54½ bushels of oats per acre from freshly broken sod. Send on your reports and samples.

The settlers along the Dawson Road have had good crops. Messrs McQuade, Wright, Nesbit, Robertson and Dunlop, report wheat, oats, and barley, fully up to the average of our report. Settlers here have good stacks of hay saved, and are realizing cash therefor at good prices. A considerable breaking of land is being done, so that next year the area sown will probably be double that of this season. Prairie chickens are tolerably plentiful, but rather wild.

The Messrs. McIvor, of Greenwood, were in town, Tuesday, and report that their threshing machine has put through this season 35,000 bushels of grain. It is now working at Portage la Prairie, where most all the threshers of the Province are gathered. They also report, in their opinion, that of all the grain they have threshed, wheat will average 35 bushels to the acre; barley, 50 bushels; and oats 75. Of wheat they have threshed as high as 50 bushels to the acre. The best wheat will be kept for seed.

To the Editor of the Free Press.

The threshing machines are busy here now, and I send you the following, which I vouch for :—

My neighbour, Mr. Wm. McLeod, sowed twelve bushels of oats upon six acres of land, and threshed six hundred bushels of good oats, full measure. The oats stood uncut fully ten days after they were ripe. As his wheat and oats both came in together, the oats must have shaken at least eight bushels to each acre. His wheat averaged thirty-four bushels to the acre. Mr. Donald McKay threshed 1,100 bushels of oats from ten and a half acres of land. I could name many who threshed from ninety to one hundred bushels to the acre. I would like to know if there is any other place in this Province, I may add in the Dominion, that can beat High Bluff! If so, have the figures sent on. The above is perfectly reliable.

JAMES WHIMSTER.

Dec. 27th, 1876.

About the good crops in Manitoba, the Toronto *Mail* has the following cheering words :—" This is a year of abundant crops in Manitoba. Mr. J. C. Smith, of Sessions, Cooper & Smith, Toronto, returned the other day from a visit to the Prairie Province, and reports that the yield there this year is splendid. He saw fields of oats and timothy hay averaging five feet in height, and we have been shown samples of oats, wheat, and barley, given him by Mr. William Mars, of High Bluff, which indicate a most luxuriant growth. The average this year is placed at seventy bushels per acre for oats, and fifty bushels per acre for wheat and barley. He found, on the 3rd of August, turnips growing from seed sown two months before, that had then reached the circumference of eighteen, twenty, and twenty-two inches. The samples of Manitoba grain referred to, picked, while growing, may be seen in the office of the firm, on Front street. The large crop of this year cannot fail to give Manitoba a start, and the date when the new Province will have produce for exportation is evidently now rapidly drawing near."

Everywhere throughout the country the busy hum of the threshing machine is heard, and the farmers are jubilant over the results. Notwithstanding the unusually trying harvest the crops in many cases are turning out very fine. In a recent drive through the townships of east Red River we noticed a specially good sample of wheat passing through the machine on the place of Mr. Forbes, his crop of 600 bushels averaging thirty bushels to the acre. Messrs. Tuson, Macdonald, James Archibald, Corbett, Ogilvie, and others, of Springfield, report very fine grains, with yield fully up to the average reported. Oats and barley are generally of unusually fine quality and productiveness. Mr. George Miller, of Cook's Creek, on a sowing of two acres of fresh broken sod, reaped eighty bushels of first-class oats. Mr. Fullerton reports a fine yield of hulless oats. Mr. W. J. Allan has some fine grains of Montana rye and wheat of good promise from a few seeds sent to him from Montana last spring. Messrs. Ross and Ede, and in fact all the farmers of Sunnyside, are well satisfied with their splendid prospects for the future. The country everywhere presents a novel and gratifying appearance, in being dotted with stacks of grain in every direction the eye may turn. Farmers, though selling a load or two of wheat at the present prices for immediate necessity, are inclined to hold the bulk of their crops for a dollar per bushel.

MANITOBA HAY.

The weather remains fair and warm, and the season of Indian summer seems likely to continue late into the fall. Even now a few of the dawdlers in husbandry have but just carted the last of their hay, and had the season continued stormy and wet some of the cattle would have fared lightly during the winter months off even the dry and stalky stuff which has last been taken from the ground. It is a fact but little appreciated by the practical farmers, though well known amongst their more scientific brethren, that the earliest grass crop, cut when in flower or when the seed is just forming, yields a far more nutritious, though less bulky, food, than the more mature produce; and that the same stock will thrive better and keep in better condition—and with less waste—on the average yield of the younger and sweeter hay, than they will on the older and coarser feed, taken after the sap has subsided and the saccharine matter has hardened into seed.

The hay crop is of the most luxuriant character, and is now ready to cut. The legal date for entering on public land to cut hay is the 15th of July.

MANITOBA FRUIT.

Strawberries and green peas and new potatoes are amongst the luxuries that can be found in some private households.—*July* 1, 1876.

Large quantities of blueberries are brought into the city and readily disposed of at from fifteen to eighteen cents a quart.—*July* 29, 1876.

A hundred pounder water melon is to be found in Hon. James McKay's garden. This is good news for the boys.

There is an abundance of strawberries in the country this year, far exceeding the produce of former seasons.—*July* 29, 1876.

Strawberries are in the market, and sell at twenty-five cents a quart.

WOOL-GROWING IN MANITOBA.

Our attention has of late been drawn to the fine texture and length of wool produced in this Province; and from inquiry we learn that sheep, as far as they have been tried, are here almost, if not entirely, free from disease—the mutton is of good quality, and the fleeces heavy. This is a matter of major importance, and though we cannot overlook the value of the stock as a food producer, the value of the fleece, both for home manufacture and for export, is a consideration which will commend its production to the farmer and stock raiser; and the expansion of the small bands of sheep which now graze on the prairies into large flocks will be but the matter of a little time. This freedom from disease is doubtless due in a great measure to the usual dryness of the climate; and with a sufficiency of hay, and the natural shelter of the bluffs in the woody districts, they thrive well during the winter, and require but little care. Sheep under favourable circumstances return a large profit to their owner, and in a climate adapted to their production they usually claim a large share of attention.

MANITOBA GAME.

SPORT.—C. V. Alloway, writing from Manitoba to friends in Montreal, says: "I have just finished my fall duck hunt. The Hon. James McKay and myself in two days killed 480 large stock ducks and 103 fall ditto. We also got three large moose and any number of chickens, rabbits, etc. During my summer rambles I managed to kill three grizzly bears."

GAME.—Messrs. Wm. Chambers and Tom Chapman have returned from a trip to Lake Manitoba. They succeeded in a day and a half's shooting in bagging two hundred and thirty-five ducks and four large geese.

A party consisting of Messrs. H. G. McMicken, Robt. Woods, and S. L. Bedson brought down seven hundred and eighty-three ducks, in two day's shooting on the east side of Lake Winnipeg,

Some gentlemen who were out along the stage road to Pembina, report prairie chicken plentiful enough about twelve or fifteen miles from this city.

A gentleman who returned from Emerson, Monday, reports immense flocks of wild pigeons met with on the course of the stage road.

MANITOBA FISHERIES.

The extensive fisheries of Lakes Manitoba and Winnipegosis are now, and justly, attracting attention, and promise to be more largely worked than heretofore. Whitefish, which, from its superior quality and demand, forms the chief fishing, may be said to come into season on or about the 15th Aug., then they are fat and firm and in prime order; later in the fall they are of inferior quality, although they again improve towards the spring, and are by some considered to be better in quality in the early fall. The chief takes are at present made along the western shore of Lake Manitoba, at Big Point, Sandy Bay, and Manitoba Post, also at Big Sandy Point, where some ten nets are worked the year round. Gold-eyes are taken in abundance in the Fairford river, and at Salt Point in Lake Winnipegosis, the annual take of whitefish is very large. The occupation is also pursued to advantage around several of the islands, and many of the best fishing grounds in the upper lakes are at present not at all or but partially worked, and this is owing in a great measure to the uncertain and inefficient means of lake communication. The average weight of the whitefish may be taken at about three pounds, and as such they are valued in the neighbourhood of the fisheries at from two to three cents each, while in the southern settlements the large and constant demand for them is ill and sparsely supplied at from twelve to twenty cents each. The development of the trade only awaits the establishment of a suitable depot or depots at some easily accessible point on the southern shore of the lake, to which the early fall fish may be taken in bulk, and where they may be dried, smoked and salted, or otherwise cured as may be deemed suitable for the market, and thence supplied to the consumer.

WILD HOPS AND RICE.

Wild hops abound in the woods and bush, and are being gathered for sale and domestic use; the wild rice along the river and lake shore will also shortly be ripe.

STOCK-RAISING IN MANITOBA.

A letter from Manitoba to the Sarnia *Observer*, dated June 6th, says:—"The feed on the prairie is splendid just now. Cattle can fill themselves in an hour's time ; the grass, in fact, being waving everywhere in the breeze. The land here is very easily worked, when once you take a crop off it. There is, in fact, no trick at all in cultivating it ; but if water was always as plentiful as it is just now, there would be very little farming done, as people would content themselves with keeping cattle. I could keep a hundred head easily, as I could, with a mower and sulky rake, cut and save all the hay they would consume in the winter, within two miles of my door, as there is a vast hay marsh stretching away to White Mud River ; and as for feed for them in the summer, it is in the greatest abundance."

A letter from Mr. John W. Parker, of Headingly, to Mr. John Hood, of Dalhousie, is published, from which we select the following items that may be found interesting here :—

"The Province's resources for agriculture and stock-raising are unbounded, and beyond what most of you Dalhousie people could imagine. I am cutting barley now which I sowed on the 1st of June, which will yield nearly sixty bushels to the acre. I planted potatoes about May 10th, and sold the new potatoes (nearly full grown) on the 12th or 14th of July, in Winnipeg at $2, to $2.50 per bushel.

"There is no better stock-raising country on the American continent but for the long winter and the hay making ; but there is plenty of wild hay of an excellent quality to be had for all present wants, and nearly every one cuts hay and grain by machinery here, so that we cut it cheaper and easier than you do in Dalhousie. My two men (Wm. Robinson, from Lavant Lake, and Samuel McIntyre, from Almonte) cut 100 tons this year, and had it done in time for harvest. We used four oxen for cutting and raking, and let the horses run idle. We find oxen just as good, nearly as quick, and far cheaper than horses. We have oxen here which will walk as fast as any common span of horses, and they work double or single in trains, or cart harness all the same.

MANITOBA A GOOD MARKET FOR THOROUGH-BRED STOCK.

This season's crop is now apparently so certain to be a large return, and the area sown is so great, that farmers will this fall be enabled to go into the purchase of stock more largely. The special advantages which the rich natural grasses of this country offer for cattle raising, is leading many to turn their attention to it. Those who have already invested in cattle have found it especially advantageous, yet at no time have the markets of the city been fully supplied, and in consequence poor, lank, and worn-out working ox meat is readily sold at the price of Christmas beef in Ontario. Indeed, so limited is the supply of the cattle in the country, that droves from Minnesota and Iowa have a practical monopoly of our market, and with milch cows at $30 to $40, and working oxen at $130 to $150 a yoke, it is no doubt a profitable trade. Little has been done towards the introduction of thoroughbred stock, from want of surplus capital in the hands óf our farmers, though they are fully alive to the importance of the subject, and undoubtedly would, singly or in neighborhoods, be ready to invest in such if brought in for sale. It has been suggested by some of our leading farmers that if some enterprising breeder, either in Ontario or Minnesota, would try our market once, they would find the speculation a very profitable one, and a favourable opportunity will occur during the fall exhibition of the Provincial Agicultural Society, in this city, in October next, of meeting all the farmers of the North-West, at a time when their bank accounts will be in the best possible condition. A word to the wise, etc., etc.

CHRISTMAS MARKETS.—N. P. Clarke's stall was handsomely decorated for the holidays, and the manager, Israel Johnston, made a most tempting display of Christmas stall-fed beef, raised by Mr. Alexander Adams, of Clear Springs. The animal dressed tipped the beam at 1,062 lbs. Some fine Manitoba mutton, purchased from John Bourke, St. James, were shown, three sheep averaging 85 lbs., dressed ; and there were turkeys, geese, chickens and oysters till you can't rest.

EASTER BEEF.—Mr. Rocan made a fine display of Easter beef. One animal, a fine cow weighing nearly eleven hundred, was stall-fed by Mr. John Higgins, and was purchased from him at a good round figure.

IMPORTATION OF LIVE STOCK FROM UNITED STATES AND CANADA.

(*Wilmar Republican Gazette.*)

The **chief feature of** our monthly fair on Saturday was the **unprecedented array of** beef cattle, oxen, steers and cows, though but few **of the latter.** Fifty head came in from Benville county, but the **major** portion of the stock was fatted in this county. Upwards of two hundred head were sold during the day to Brackett, Elliot & Co., of Minneapolis, who intend to take them to Fort Garry. The drove, numbering three hundred and ten head, left on Monday for the aforesaid point.

Bill Smith arrived on Saturday night with two hundred and fifty-three fat cattle in fine condition, and which will go a good way towards supplying the tables of hungry Winnipeggers during the coming winter.

T. J. Demers, of Montana, left this city by boat last Friday, highly satisfied with his sale of horses and cattle. He intends returning to Winnipeg early next spring, with two thousand head of cattle and four hundred head of horses.

Large droves of cattle keep coming in from Minnesota, and meet with ready sale at prices that seem to satisfy the drovers. latest rates are: three year old steers, $30 to $40; four year old, $35 to $50; oxen, $150 to $180 per yoke; milch cows. $35 to $50. Good animals meet with ready sale.

STOCK FROM THE WEST.—Mr. T. J. Demers, recently arrived in this city from Frenchtown, Montana. He with a party of eight, left that place on the 13th April, with ninety horses and six hundred and seventy head of cattle. About twenty of the latter and a few horses were lost.

Several large droves of cattle and flocks of sheep passed through Moorhead last week, headed for the British possessions.

Another instalment of fat and working cattle—three hundred head—have arrived from Uncle Sam's dominions for N. P. Clarke, who is represented here by Isaac Johnston.

STOCK COMING.—Mr. L. Worthington started from Sauk Centre recently, with a drove of one hundred and twenty-five cattle and six hundred sheep for the Manitoba markets.

Droves of cattle are expected in shortly from Minnesota.

The first importation of Berkshire pigs was made Sunday, by Mr. J. Dent. The pigs were brought in from St. Thomas, Ontario.

Large droves of cattle are passing Pembina almost daily, and nearly a thousand sheep have passed during the last fortnight.

A drove of two hundred and sixty-five head of cattle passed through Fargo recently from Stearns County, Minn., bound for Winnipeg.

Two droves of cattle, one, eighty-two head, and the other, two hundred head, passed through Fargo this week for Winnipeg, from Southern Minnesota.

The above will give some idea of the business to be done in Manitoba, in the way of stock-raising.

WELL BRED STOCK REQUIRED IN MANITOBA.

Extract from the report of the Directors of the Provincial Agricultural Society:—

"It would be highly desirable if a greater degree of attention were given to the raising of cattle, hogs, sheep, etc., as the wants of new settlers, government working parties, police, etc., will for some years furnish a profitable local market, and its supply will retain in the country large sums which are now sent abroad. The supply of choice breeds would be a legitimate object for the enterprise of your society ; but inasmuch as your resources will not at present admit of it, the matter must be left to private enterprise, to be suggested and encouraged by the members of your society who may correspond with stock-breeders, informing them that such shipments would meet with remunerative sale here, especially at the time of our annual exhibition.

FARMING IN MANITOBA.

A Mr. Lewis arrived here Saturday before last ; was out to see a farm on Monday ; on Tuesday he had concluded its purchase, and on Wednesday had planted potatoes on some broken ground, and now is erecting a house. That is the kind of men Manitoba wants and the kind of men who want Manitoba, and who will in a few years be counted lucky. Pluck and common sense it is, only.

A contract for cutting and threshing one field of oats, not many miles distant from this city, was recently let for $1,200. This will give an idea of what farming is in the Prairie Province.

EARLY.—Mr. Jas. Jefferson, of Greenwood, commenced ploughing on the 10th April.

Ploughing has been commenced in Springfield, Rockwood, and other parts of the Province.—*22nd April*, 1876.

MANITOBA DAIRY PRODUCE.

The large competition in the butter class—there being over eighty entries—and the invariable good quality of the exhibits, would have been remarkable in older countries, and mark the fact that this Province is one of the best dairy countries in the world.

CONTEMPLATED CHEESE FACTORY—A GOOD OPENING IN MANITOBA.

CHEESE FACTORY.—A Mr. Colwell, from Ontario, contemplates starting a cheese factory next spring near Grosse Isle. This gentleman is in the business in that Province, and will move his establishment hither.—*Dec. 30th*, 1876.

IMPORTATION OF BUTTER FROM UNITED STATES.

A heavy shipment of butter—two tons—has just been imported from Minnesota by Snyder & Anderson. It is also to be hoped before long Manitoba will be able to produce a sufficient supply of this commodity.

MANITOBA FUR TRADE.

Furs—Messrs. Kew, Stobart & Co., made the first shipment of their furs, amounting to about $15,000, Monday. They also sent out 205 bales of buffalo robes.

The "Manitoba" took out three hundred and sixty-three bales of furs Friday evening.

An immense quantity of furs is stored in the old Pacific Hotel building.

MANITOBA TRADE.

Taking the crop report of Manitoba published, in this paper for its text, the London *Advertiser* says : "Those already settled in the country (Manitoba) stand a good chance to get rich by selling food to the new immigrants, and immigration will keep pace with increased grain-growing, so that by the time there is a surplus for exportation there will be a railway outlet by Thunder Bay and another by the American Railway system. Coarse grains can all be used with profit for fattening meat for the home market, which has been supplied almost entirely by importation, not for the want of stock so much as the want of grain to bring the same to fair slaughtering condition."

Country Produce.—It is very gratifying for persons interested in the growth of this city to note the changed aspect of affairs on the street as compared with last fall. Now, on fine days, Main Street is crowded with teams laden with all kinds of agricultural and dairy produce, wool, hay, &c., for which the owners receive good prices—mostly cash—and in consequence, city quadrupeds and bipeds are more highly fed than ever in this new country. Wednesday we noticed on the streets, farmers from the Rosseau, Woodlands, the Boyne, Grassmere, Greenwood, Cook's Creek, Scratching River, Springfield; and in fact nearly every settlement in the Province was represented. Our merchants are buying liberally the products of the farmers, and the latter are thereby enabled to pay off their debts, which places them in a good position for next season's operations.—*Dec. 9th*, 1876.

In referring to this Province it says : "Manitoba is the youngest Province in the Dominion, but by no means the least

6

promising. Its trade is steadily augmenting. The total value thereof in 1876 was $2,505,615, of which $1,735,427 were imports, and $770,188 exports. The latter, up to this time, have been chiefly furs. Its imports are largely obtained from Ontario and Quebec, and are familiar to our mercantile friends. Manitoba, and the North-West generally promise to prove, before many years, a valuable field for Canadian manufactures."

The fur market opened dull and inactive, but within a few days past heavy sales have been made at good prices. In this article a new system has been inaugurated, and is found to work well. Instead of buying by the bale, unexamined, at an average price per robe, the bales are opened, and every hide valued and paid for according to quality.

The immensity of the Manitoba trade is evidenced by the fact that the Ontario steamers are heavily laden every trip with goods for this Province, and one steamer lately had to leave three hundred tons for another boat to bring.

The amount of business transacted in Winnipeg is really astonishing. One can form no conception of its extent unless he has ocular demonstration of the fact. Some idea may have been formed by the allusion in my former communication to the customs' receipts and steamboat traffic, but, to be convinced of its magnitude, one must really see it.

Of course the reader will very naturally say, How can this be? whence all this business? there are only some thirty thousand souls in the whole Province, and why this amount of business to supply this mere handful with the common necessaries of life. But, dear reader, the home business proper is a mere beginning of the gross trade of Winnipeg. Why, sir, the open prairie surrounding the city, while I was there, was literally covered with the tents and carts of the inland travellers; the streets literally crowded with the ever creaking Red River carts, and the stores and taverns were filled with the variegated crowd that owned them, throwing their money about in a way which indicated that they were bound to make things generally agreeable as long as it lasted.

The following is clipped from the *Globe's* English correspondence: "The advancing trade of Winnipeg, a few years ago a little village, cannot be better shown than in the fact that a merchant is now in London making large purchases for shipment to Winnipeg direct. It is impossible in the face of facts, to shut one's eyes to the growing importance of the Prairie Province."

BONDED GOODS. The proposed change in the Dominion tariff is causing quite a flutter among the merchants. One paid a bill of $2,500 the other day on his stock of bonded goods; others are still awaiting definite advices from Ottawa. The aggregate amount of duties which will be paid in here at once, if the tariff takes effect, will not be less than $30,000—a pretty good show for a "pauper" city.—*February* 19, 1876.

FOR THE OLD COUNTRY.—Gerrie & "Willie" were among the passengers this morning for the East. Gerrie, we understand, is homeward bound—with the object of purchasing largely for the Indian and jobbing trade, of which this city is the centre. We beg to notify the shrewd inhabitants of the Granite City, that notwithstanding an absence of 40 years from his native Aberdeen, they will make a mistake if they regard him as another Rip Van Winkle. All we can say is, we wish him s'ccess and *bon voyage*.

MANITOBA FREIGHT.—The Moorhead *Star* says:— " Enormous quantities of freight consigned down the river and bound west to Montana and Bismarck, continue to arrive here. It is estimated that 2,000 tons of Manitoba freight are now in the yards here, with large daily arrivals. One day alone 600 tons of flour for river transhipment were received. The steamers take all that the stage of water will allow, and yet the accommodations are great."

Staticians of the eastern provinces would be surprised to see invoices of 1,600 pairs of blankets, 300 pieces of wincey, 300 dozen hose, and like quantities throughout a large stock for a business house in the four year old city of Winnipeg. Most of our houses now import directly from the manufacturers in England and Scotland, and next year it is likely all will do so.

The amount of duties in Manitoba for the year ending 30th June, 1876, was $253,045.88, as against $171,430.86 in 1875, and $67,471.97 in 1874.

FOR ENGLAND.—Mr. John O. LeCappellaine started for England this morning, where he goes to purchase goods for Mr. J. H. Ashdown's spring trade.

HARD TIMES.—One of our city clothing stores took in fifteen hundred dollars over the counter one day last week.

A train of sixty carts, laden with furs purchased by Mr. Bannatyne and Mr. Patterson, passed up Main Street, Wednesday.

TRADE WITH THE INTERIOR.

Up to this date over 1,500 carts laden with supplies, goods, etc., have been sent west from this city on Government account to the various mounted police posts. It is estimated that about 2,000 more have gone out on private account for traders, telegraph contractors, and the Hudson Bay Company; and three months of the season is yet left.

Travellers from the west report that traders parties are strung all along the road, coming to the capital for their yearly market. It is expected that on account of the large catch this season, their purchase of goods will be large.

A heavy order has been received by Mr. J. H. Ashdown from the Hudson's Bay Company for tin-ware for outlying posts. Among the articles are 3,000 tin pails, 1,300 round pans, 1,500 oval pans, 1,800 pint cups, 1,500 half-pint cups, and 400 teapots. The amount of the order will be about $3,000.

Mr. Owen E. Hughes, of the firm of Kew, Stobart & Co., who left here last summer for a trading trip towards the setting sun, has succeeded in establishing a trading post at Cross Lake, one hundred miles north of Norway House, and about five hundred miles from Winnipeg, where he is doing an extensive business. He has sent in an order for a large amount of goods, with part of which a train started on Thursday, and the remainder will be shipped shortly.

A large number of carts, laden with freight, will leave in a few days for Fort Ellice, Shoal Lake, etc., on Government account.

The amount of goods going west from this city must be enormous in the aggregate, as nearly every day trains of carts laden with merchandize are sent out.

AGRICULTURAL MACHINERY.

We understand that Mr. James Barclay, of Stony Mountain, the contractor for the new penitentiary, intends erecting a foundry and agricultural implement manufactory on the river front, near McLane's Mill, on land purchased from the H. B. Co. We congratulate Mr. Barclay upon his determination to remain and invest his capital here in this much needed and undoubtedly remunerative enterprise.

The wire and castings for one hundred fanning mills, being manufactured here by Dick & Banning, were brought in by the Manitoba, and the mills will be finished this week.

About two hundred reapers and mowers have already been sold this season by the implement dealers of this city. One firm, Dick & Banning, have disposed of eighty-three machines.

MANITOBA WHEAT FOR SEED.

On this point we have the opinion of a very high authority on the subject, viz: J. W. Taylor, Esq., U.S. Consul at Winnipeg; than whom no man has studied the subject with closer attention. He says, "that on a recent visit to the east he was surprised to find that Minnesota spring wheat, when forwarded and sold separately in the eastern market, commanded ten per cent. more than wheat of Canada and New York State. Further, that spring wheat raised on the line of the Northern Pacific, and St. Paul and Pacific railroads, brought five cents per bushel more than the same wheat raised 150 miles further south." His inference is that Manitoba wheat, when there shall be a surplus over local consumption, will bring 15c per bushel premium; almost enough to cover transport to Montreal or New York. This appreciation in price is owing to the increase in weight and gluten of the flour, attributable to the northern climate, and other favourable circumstances. Manitoba wheat is already in demand as a desirable change of seed in the adjoining States, and the Department of Agriculture at Washington proposes to distribute 200 bushels in small quantities over the United States.

MILLS IN MANITOBA.

CROPS AND MILLS.—Mr. W. Smith, miller, of Portage la Prairie, is in the city. He reports barley nearly all cut, and oats far advanced in cutting. He saw three fields of oats cut on Wednesday near the stage road. Crops everywhere north, west and east of Portage la Prairie are magnificent, and will give an unprecedently large yield; the loss by drowning is very insignificant, the worst managed farm showing a better growth than a model farm in Ontario. Mr. Smith is adding another run of stones and a new boiler to his mill at Portage la Prairie, making now three run with a capacity for grinding 1,000 bushels in twenty-four hours. His Mill at Point de Chene is being pushed to completion, and will be ready for grinding early in the fall.

From Mr. Smith we have obtained his estimate of the grinding capacity of the mills of the Province for this season's harvest :—

Palestine, C. P. Brown,	1 run
Totogan, Chisholm & Bubar,	1 "
Portage la Prairie, Wm. Smith,	3 "
St. Norbert, J. Lemay,	3 "
Point de Chene, Wm. Smith,	1 "
Winnipeg, J. W. Mc Lane,	4 "
" Bassett & McMillen,	2 "
St. Paul's Parish, H. Pritchard,	2 "
St. Andrew's, E. H. G. G. Hay,	2 "
Mapleton, Hudson's Bay Company,	1

This makes a total of twenty runs of stone with a grinding capacity of 4,000 bushels per day.

The people of the extreme western settlements are much pleased with the convenience which Mr. C. P. Brown's new mill at Gladstone is affording them. It is turning out a first-class article of flour and giving universal satisfaction. The mill is one of the Waterous Engine Works Co.'s, of Brantford, twenty-horse power portable saw and grist mill combined, which Mr. Brown purchased last summer. We learn that he had no trouble in erecting the mill, it having been all set up at the works, and marked before taking apart, which, with the plan sent with it, avoided all trouble.

ANOTHER MILL.—Mr. James Spence, of this city, has purchased the remains of the Tait mill at Silver Heights, and imported new machinery including two runs of stones, and is now engaged in the erection of a first-class grist mill on the Mirey Creek, just east of the Manitoba Brewery, which he expects to have in running order by the first of October next.

A new grist mill has recently been erected in the heart of the Mennonite settlement, about fifteen miles from Rat River. It is a two and a half storey building, 26x34, and has one run of stone, the motive power being supplied by a twelve horsepower engine. The builders are Messrs. Maud & Co., of Berlin, Ont., and the machinery was procured from Gouldie & McCollough, of Galt. The mill will cost about $4,000, and is expected to be in running order shortly. Mr. Weins, a Mennonite, is the proprietor.

At McMillan & Bassett's mills 2,400 bushels of wheat are at present ground every week; but with the new boiler which is being put in, the quantity will be increased to 3,000 bushels.

An excellent sample of flour from the Marquette Milling Co., Portage la Prairie, stated by competent judges to be equal to any XXXX in the market, has been brought into the city. This mill is running full time, and a large quantity of its flour is finding its way here.

A third run of stone is being put into Billy Smith's mill at the Portage. The mill is now running night and day.

McLane's Mill is now busy filling a large order for flour for the Mennonites. Five hundred sacks were sent out Tuesday.

Four hundred bushels of wheat were delivered in two hours recently at McMillan & Bassett's mill, for custom work alone.

Twelve lots were recently purchased at the Town of Selkirk, by Mr. Martin Hoover, of Port Elgin, Ontario, who intends erecting on the property a large grist mill of four run of stones. Mr. Hoover left for Ontario yesterday to complete the necessary arrangements.

Selkirk is to have a new grist and steam saw mill and sash and door factory. Messrs. McCroskrie & Thomas have the matter in hand, and intend pushing the business to its fullest extent.

The saw mill of Mr. Alex. McArthur, on the Winnipeg river, has been purchased by Messrs. Thompson & Walkley.

STILL ANOTHER.—McKay & Smith's mill at the Pointe de Chene will be in working order this week.

Another run of stone is being put in place at McLane's mill.

CITY OF WINNIPEG.

WINNIPEG, AS SEEN BY A STRANGER.—Mr. Warring Kennedy, a prominent Toronto merchant, who paid a visit to Winnipeg recently, thus gives his impression of this city in the columns of a Toronto paper :

" The City of Winnipeg is the door through which immigration into the Province of Manitoba must pass, and is the great distributing point, not only for the Province, but for the whole North-West territory. It is situated at the confluence of the Red and Assiniboine rivers, on the west bank of the former, at an elevation of thirty feet above water level. Only a few years ago it was merely a village, containing some dozen of houses. In 1872. the population was 300, now it is 6,000. This rate of increase in four years has been equal to that of Chicago's early days in ten years. In 1830, the population of the latter was only 70 ; in 1840, it was 4,470, although it now has 300,-000. This growth of the City of Winnipeg, as may be expected, has favoured the development of property, and some have become rich by merely investing their savings in cheap city lots. Many lots bought three years ago for fifty dollars, are now worth five hundred. At present, suburban lots are considered the best investment. This growth, although rapid, has not been unhealthy."

PROGRESS IN THE NORTH-WEST.

The following letter from the Bishop of Saskatchewan is addressed to the London *Free Press :*—

DEAR SIR,—I reached this place on Tuesday, the 18th inst. —not quite a week from London, Ont. I could not help contrasting the speed of this journey with the comparatively long period of upwards of three weeks that was required to complete the same distance when I with my family came to Red River from London, just ten years ago. I have now before me the printed copy of a letter I sent on my arrival to my old friend Mr. Siddons, then the editor of the *Prototype*. It was there stated that we came *via* Milwaukee, Prairie du Chien and the Mississippi to St. Paul, where we stayed a few days and then went on to St. Cloud, the farthest point we could travel by rail or steamer. From that to Fort Abercrombie, a distance of 180 miles, we travelled by stage, at 60 miles a day, passing through the section of country that was the scene of the Indian massacre of 1862. At Fort Abercrombie we commenced our

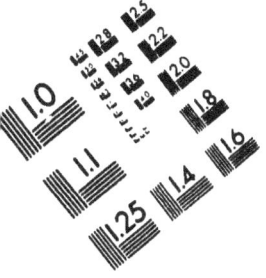 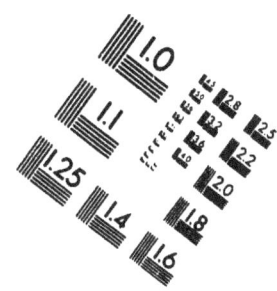

**IMAGE EVALUATION
TEST TARGET (MT-3)**

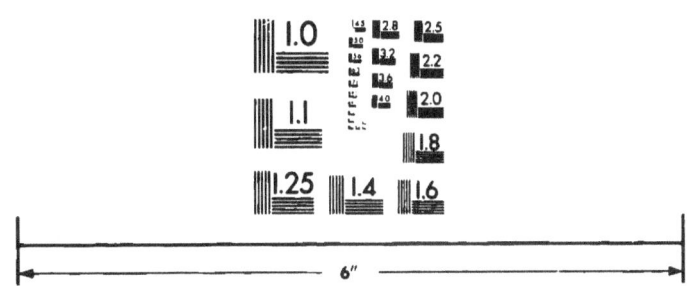

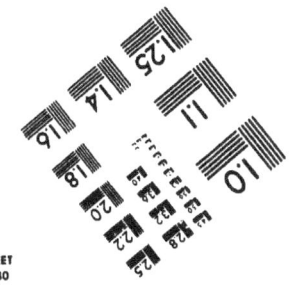

Photographic
Sciences
Corporation

23 WEST MAIN STREET
WEBSTER, N.Y. 14580
(716) 872-4503

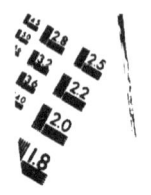

prairie journey with the covered waggons and carts. It occupied us in all seven and a half days.

What a change has taken place in these ten years! I left London this month on Tuesday, the 11th, at 7 p.m., and reached Fisher's Landing, at Red Lake River, on Saturday, at 10 p.m., where I went aboard a steamer that brought me to Fort Garry on Tuesday at 5 a.m., on the 18th inst. In that same letter to Mr. Siddons I speak of " a small village near Fort Garry with a number of stores." The small village of ten years ago is now the city of Winnipeg, with, I suppose, about six thousand inhabitants. In the energy and business enterprise of her merchants, I believe Winnipeg to be quite on a par with the most prosperous and thriving cities of the United States. Commercially speaking, I feel sure that Winnipeg has the opportunity of a splendid career before her, and she has already shown that she numbers among her population a body of men who know how to turn good opportunities to account. One illustration of the business energy of Winnipeg I find in the contrast between the state of prices there to-day and what I found ten years ago, as the following extract from the above quoted letter will show:—" All imported goods are *very dear*, owing to their having to be carried over the prairies in carts. Some things required for household use are two, three, and four times as dear as in Canada."

At the present moment my impression is that groceries and dry goods of the best quality can be procured in Winnipeg at about as low a figure as in Ontario.

There is every prospect of a magnificent crop in Manitoba. As yet there is no appearance of grasshoppers, as far as I can learn.

Very faithfully yours,
J. SASKATCHEWAN.

St. Andrew's, Manitoba, July 26, 1876.

This is what the correspondent of an Ottawa paper thinks of the Prairie City:—" A stranger's first impression on arriving at Winnipeg is, that it is a dull, dreary place, but a walk through the principal streets completely disabuses his mind of that fallacy, and convinces him that there is not a livelier place of its size in the whole Dominion of Canada. The amount of business done is indeed surprising. Stores are numerous, and they all seem to get plenty of custom. One thing certain is that, as in other Canadian cities, there are no failures or rumours of failures, but on the contrary, every merchant appears to be rolling up wealth. Without any exaggeration, I can say that there appears to be more business done than in Ottawa ; there is more bustle on the principal street and more evidences generally of business activity.

REAL ESTATE.

How many now in Ontario will regret forever the opportunity now passing of acquiring the best wheat lands in the world through investment in scrip ; in five years, when those lands now settled upon are worth $20 per acre, they will be purchasing ten acres for what would now purchase ten hundred.

A cash offer of $3,000 was recently made for the small lot on Main Street, next Dr. Bird's drug store—and refused.

An Ontario gentleman, now in the city, purchased a year ago the Queen's Hotel on Main Street, for $2,600, and now receives a rental therefrom of $1,100—a pretty neat return from a small investment in Winnipeg city property.—*July 29th*, 1876.

OPENING OF NAVIGATION ON RED RIVER.

THE RIVER.—Of course it is impossible to tell with any certainty the exact time when the Red River will unfasten its "icy fetters," but the probabilities are—judging from the present condition of the weather—that navigation can be resumed as soon as last year. The first steamboat to arrive at Moorhead last season was the "Selkirk," Capt. Alex. Griggs, which touched our levee at 3 p.m., Thursday, April 22nd. The first boat in 1874, arrived on April 24th, and the first in 1873, on April 26th. The state of the weather at this writing is such as to prophesy an early opening of navigation, although all conclusions must necessarily be over half guess work. The large quantity of snow now on the ground may augur a liberal quantity of flood water, which with our usual spring rains, will give a good stage of water the first part of season, at least.—Moorhead *Star, April 8th*, 1876.

"THE FIRST BOAT."—"The first boat" of the season, arrived on Tuesday, 26th inst, being the "Minnesota," having a cargo of 5,165 sacks of seed wheat for the Central Relief Committee.

This is the earliest arrival of a steamboat from the United States, ever known. The nearest approach to it was the arrival of the "Selkirk" on the 28th of April, 1871 ; and the next nearest, the arrival of the "Selkirk" on the 30th April, in 1875.—*April 29th*, 1876.

The following are the dates of the ice leaving Red River at the Stone Fort, from the journal of Wm. Flett, Esq., H. B. Co. :—1869, 19th April ; 1870, 9th April ; 1871, 24th April ; 1872, 4th May ; 1873, 27th April ; 1874, 1st May ; 1875, 28th April.

NAVIGATION OF THE SASKATCHEWAN.

A gentleman in St. Paul has written to his old home in Massachusetts, to remove the erroneous impression that prevails there that that city is the extreme North-West corner of habitable creation. He says:—"No better grain-growing country exists than extends for 500 miles north, and 600 miles west, while 1,500 miles north-west from this city, streams are open and pasturage is grown a full month earlier than here (air-line distances are meant). Nor is this vast North-West unapproachable. You can, to day, take rail from here to the Northern Pacific crossing of the Red River, and there take your choice of seven steamboats, of from 300 to 600 tons each, to Fort Garry, Manitoba, 600 miles by river, (about 280 miles by land.) At Fort Garry take a lake propeller (like those on Lake Erie and other eastern lakes) through Lake Winnipeg, 275 to 300 miles to its north-western end; then take a river steamer and go up the Saskatchewan, and its northern branch to Fort Edmonton and beyond, 1,400, or within 450 to 500 miles of the waters of the Pacific Ocean, and when you get there you can go ashore and telegraph the same day to your home in the Connecticut valley or Berkshire hills. These are facts. The wires are up, and the boats are there and running."

The Rev. L. Warner, who has been for the past two years engaged in missionary work in the Saskatchewan country, has recently returned to Ontario. Mr. Warner left Victoria Mission—about twenty miles east of Edmonton—on the 26th of May, and came down by the H. B. Co's steamboat, the Northcote, to Grand Rapids, near Lake Winnipeg, where the goods are transhipped from the steamer navigating the Saskatchewan River to the boat plying between that point and the City of Winnipeg. The goods from either steamer are taken over the portage, which is four miles long, by means of a tramway which the Hudson's Bay Company has laid down.

Mr. Healy is of opinion that were the navigation of the Lake Manitoba, Winnipegosis, and South Saskatchewan route improved by the canalling necessary, some nine miles only, at High Bluff and Mossy Portage, which would allow our river steamers to ascend to the mountains, the entire trade of that magnificent country would naturally tend this way. The Manitoba Southern Railway was intended to be the first link in a chain designed to connect this country with our city, and we hope it may be proceeded with. Mr. Healy states that Fort Hamilton and Fort McLeod are about the same latitude as Fort Garry, and yet the seasons are very different, ploughing being quite possible in December, in fact their finest month is November. Though the thermometer is sometimes very low, yet the cold does not continue long, and altogether the seasons are very favourable for agriculture. Cattle feed out all winter and fatten on the rich grasses, and the only objection to sheep-farming on an extensive scale is the presence of wolves. Our space limits our remarks on this interesting subject, but we may revert to it again.

The "Colvill," H. B. Co's steamer, Captain Hackland, arrived at the Lower Fort on Saturday, the 21st ult., from Grand Rapids, having made her last trip to that place for this season. She brought in about twenty-five passengers, including Capt. Aymond and his family, and the crew of the Saskatchewan steamer " Northcote." Amongst other freight were two teams belonging to the H. B. Co. The " Colville " has been laid up for the winter about five miles below the Lower Fort.

STAGE FROM MOORHEAD TO WINNIPEG.

The stages commenced running on fast time, Thursday, through to Moorhead in thirty-six hours. The mails will arrive between four and six o'clock in the mornings, instead of in the evenings, as formerly.

STAGE FROM WINNIPEG TO PORTAGE LA PRAIRIE.

Mr. Blake, of Blake & Lyons, Portage la Prairie, has purchased the stage line between Winnipeg and that place, and is now in the city to purchase horses, etc. He intends re-stocking the line, and making it really a first-class one.

EMERSON.

It may be well to preface the following statement of building improvements made in Emerson during the past summer, by the remark that Emerson is but two years old, the first building being put up in June, 1874. Considering the drawbacks to emigration in the North-West during the past year or two, the growth of this place may be considered remarkable, and an indication that it has very superior advantages as a business point. Such a start as Emerson has obtained previous to the completion of the railroads which will terminate there, insures a rapid progress when the rails are down. It may be observed that the buildings put up, though not very costly, are of a permanent character, none of them log buildings, but built of sawn lumber, with shingle roofs, and most of them well plastered. Nor are they huddled together as observable in some new western towns, but placed as if inviting the erection of other and more imposing buildings in their midst. It is noticeable also that private means alone have been used to put up these buildings, the Government not yet having had occasion to build. The cost of these buildings foots up upwards of thirty thousand dollars.

FRENCH EMIGRATION FROM UNITED STATES TO MANITOBA.

From the Toronto *Globe*:—A letter from certain French Canadian settlers in the township of Letellier, Manitoba, which appeared in *Le Nouveau Monde* of the 4th inst., gives some very interesting facts connected with their experiences in the Prairie Province. The writers came from the Eastern States in May last, and are the pioneers of what they believe will be a very great emigration from these quarters to Manitoba. It was only on the 5th of June that they took up their titles to land, and for $10 each received 160 acres of what they say is land of the very first quality. As the season was rather too far advanced to hope for a good crop from land newly broken up, they received from the Government the right to put in a crop in land on the Government farm at Dufferin, which had been ploughed some time before, and was ready for seeding. Fifteen heads of families joined and planted barley, potatoes, &c. For two weeks after there was not a drop of rain, and so they feared they had lost their time and seed. In spite, however, of these fears, they were at the time of writing, certain of reaping from twenty to thirty fold.

Nineteen more French Canadian families will leave North Adams and Fall River, Massachusetts, for Manitoba in August, 1876.

A number of French Canadians in the United States have written to friends here to purchase land for them, they intending to emigrate here in the spring. *Le Métis* states that the emigration from the Western States to Manitoba will be considerable next year.

A number of French Canadians who came here from the United States last spring, are settling at Rat River.

GENERAL INFORMATION.

THREE CARD MONTE MEN.—People travelling through Minnesota cannot be too wary of scoundrels in the shape of three card monte men, with whom the railroads and steamboats are infested, and who are daily and hourly robbing the travelling community. Fisher's Landing, and the Northern Pacific, abound with these characters, and every day we are hearing of people who have been robbed by them. Our advice to travellers is to avoid every stranger who speaks of cards, no matter in what way the subject is introduced.

MANITOBA.

We have always refrained from advising intending immigrants in their selection of localities in the North-West. The most detailed information on this point can be acquired at the Land Office in Winnipeg, and immigrants, if they desire to settle in the southern portion of the Province—in which is some of the finest land in the colony—can obtain information and select their holdings immediately upon crossing the international boundary line, and without going to Winnipeg. But location depends so much upon what a man intends to do, that advice given without a knowledge of the circumstances of the person who asks it, is not of much value. There are parts of the Province which some immigrants pass by as undesirable, that others who propose to raise stock are eager to obtain. So for some men it is better to buy a holding in the settlement belt, while for others the Government homestead, which costs only ten dollars and its settlement duties, is equally advantageous. The information and advice of a friend settled in Manitoba is the most valuable that can be obtained, and an immigrant, after his arrival, need not be at any expense, while prosecuting his inquiries, for house-rent or forage. A tent supplies the one and the prairie the other. But it should be remembered that when the winter comes employment in Manitoba ceases, and the immigrant who may have worked hard in fencing and breaking land, raising a house for himself and buildings for his animals, has a long winter to pull through, and for the first year cannot, of course, derive much from his farm. But there must always be some difficulty in making a fresh start in a new country ; and if, as is generally believed, Manitoba has not to fear the return of the grasshopper for some years, a farmer who, having his own choice of locality, fails to make a comfortable living, will have less ability than hundreds of the old settlers who never learned the principle of farming. —*From the Globe.*

LETTER FROM MANITOBA.

The following well-written and interesting letter on Manitoba affairs was received from Mr. Robert Ferguson, formerly of Grey, by Mr. Mark Cardiff, of Brussels, who has kindly handed it to us for publication. Its contents will be perused with interest by our readers. The letter is dated the 19th of January, and is addressed to Mr. Cardiff. It reads as follows :—

DEAR SIR,—Thinking that a smattering of Manitoba affairs would be interesting to you, I proceed to give you a few facts concerning this "land of grasshoppers," that I have gathered during my short stay here. Upon entering Winnipeg, after our protracted journey over the Dawson Route, I was somewhat astonished to find a town of about 6,000 inhabitants, which for stir and business fairly eclipses any of your Ontario towns of the same population. A number of excellent brick buildings have been put up during last summer. The new post office is a stately edifice, and is quite an ornament to the town. The brick, which is made in the vicinity of the town, is handsome and of a superior quality. Any person taking a tour through this Province, could not fail to be delighted with the many promising features which it presents. Its rich prairie soil, free from every obstacle that would impede the progress of agriculture, and many bluffs of timber which makes the best of wood, and can be procured by most of the farmers without going many steps from his door, make it all that can be desired for farming. Last Monday, Mr. Broadfoot and I went west about four miles to the timber limits. We travelled all the afternoon in a dense forest, as level as a floor. Most of the timber is first-class building material, and all of it the best of rail timber. All the farmers in Palestine can get all the stove wood they require almost at their door, and only have to go four or five miles for building and rail timber, while some have these conveniences right at hand.—*From the Seaforth Expositor.*

MANITOBA.

EMERSON, MANITOBA, Dec. 31st, 1875.

As many friends in Lennox and Addington have expressed a desire to know more about Manitoba and "The Great North-West," I now write to them through the columns of your valuable paper. I have been here about two months, and can form an idea of the country, its people, prospects, &c. I can truly say that the land is vast beyond conception. God alone knows all about it; just think of plains in British America with an area of 295,000 square miles, stretching from the Lake of the Woods to the Rocky Mountains and from the United States boundary to the Arctic Ocean. Manitoba is but a small part of this immense region. There are three vast steppes or prairies, the one rising above the other until they reach their western limits at the base of the Rocky Mountains. The Red River Valley, one of the three, has an area of 55,600 square miles. Of this, the Lakes Winnipeg, Winnipegosis, Manitoba, Cedar, and St. Martins occupy about 13,900 square miles. It is the most fertile of all the plains of the west, and easiest of access to a people coming in from the east. Supposing that the half of this or 3,400 square miles of this (2,176,000 acres) were sown with wheat, even at the average of Minnesota, seventeen bushels to the acre, the crops of the Red River Valley would be almost 41,000,000 of bushels. A field on the Pembina River, near this, which this year escaped the grasshoppers, yielded 1,800 bushels or 45 to the acre.

As to climate, I have found the winter clear, dry, and pleasant. It is colder than some parts of Ontario, but on account of the dry atmosphere it is not so much felt. It is very healthy; women having poor health in Ontario often become strong and vigorous out here. Stouter, healthier children, I never saw anywhere. I have not seen a funeral since coming here. Spring opens about as soon as on the Bay of Quinté. Winter sets in about the beginning of November. The fall of snow is much lighter here than on the St. Lawrence. We have just enough to make good sleighing. For four years the country has been swept by grasshoppers, but God who sent them can just as easily take them away. The impression here is that they will not return for a series of years. If so, there will be a great emigration westwards. Let people come; there is a stretch of one thousand miles from this to Peace River yet to be possessed. Wheat and barley ripened there this season on the 12th of August. In the Peace River Valley there are millions of acres ready for the plough. At Bow River, 800 miles west of here, there are plains where cattle can graze all winter. This place is on the great highway. Seven steamboats with barges pass weekly, and in one season 400 flatboats with cargoes valued at $5,000 each passed down from Minnesota to Winnipeg. Lest I weary your readers I will stop here. Any parties wishing further information I will be happy to aid. My address is Emerson, Manitoba.

JOHN SCOTT,
Pres. Missionary.

—*Napanee Beaver.*

Mr. Lillies, of West Pilkington, has received a letter from Manitoba, where four of his sons have been for some time. They say:—Don't fear of us starving in Manitoba; we are doing better than we could do in Ontario despite the ravages made by the grasshoppers. Two of us have cleared one hundred and sixty dollars per month all summer, burning lime and selling it at 45c per bushel, another has averaged $5 per day with his team, sometimes teaming to the new Penitentiary, and sometimes working on the railroad. The fourth works at his trade—waggon-making—in Winnipeg, for $60 per month, steady employment. Our potato crop is splendid, our peas are excellent, and we had one field of wheat that suffered no intrusion from the pest. The weather is mild, prairie chickens are very numerous, and our anticipations as regards a good time next year are big.—*Galt Reporter.*

THE GREAT NORTH-WEST.

Professor Macoun, the Government Botanist, was examined at great length by the Committee on Immigration at Ottawa, recently. He has crossed the continent twice, and made extensive inquiries into the floral and geological formation of the North-West. He has especially visited the Peace River district, of which he speaks with the utmost enthusiasm. His description of the vast area in the interior to the north-west of Fort Garry was *couleur de rose* in every respect, yet he gave such proofs of his knowledge, that none doubted the truth of his assertions. It is generally supposed in Ontario that the country lying east of the Rocky Mountains is uninhabited by white people. This is not correct, for, under the patronage of the Hudson Bay Company, numerous settlements are springing up everywhere, and a large population quietly taking up the country. Professor Macoun, who is intimately acquainted with the geography of that region, says that settlement there is infinitely far more easy than it was in Ontario thirty or so years ago. There is but one break in the navigation from Fort Garry to Edmonton, a distance by road of 850 miles, or by water upwards of twelve hundred miles. This break is a short rapid, but both above and below it the Hudson Bay Company have steamers which ply the season throughout, there being plenty of water up to October. The Professor found that the entire district along the Peace River for a distance of seven hundred and sixty miles in a belt one hundred and fifty miles wide on each side, was as suitable for the cultivation of grain as that of Ontario. He had brought samples of wheat weighing sixty-eight pounds, and of barley weighing fifty-six pounds to the bushel. The climate was even more suitable than in Ontario, for there were no wet autumns or frost to kill the young grain. There were but two seasons—summer and winter. He said, in illustration, that on a Thursday last October, the heat was so great that he had to shelter himself by lying under a cart, while on the next Sunday winter set in in full vigour, and continued steadily. The plants he found in that region were the same as those on Lake Erie, and further discoveries satisfied him that the two areas were similar in every respect. The ice in the rivers broke up in April. Stock raising was not difficult, because the grass remained fresh and green up to the very opening of winter. He had seen thousands of acres of it three and four feet long on levels two hundred feet above the Peace River. He estimated that there was 252,000,000 acres of land in that region adapted to the growth of cereals. He had tested the temperature, and showed by figures that the average summer heat at Fort William, Fort Simpson, Edmonton, and throughout that region, was similar to that of Toronto, Montreal, and higher than that of Halifax. He was positive that the climate was uncommonly suitable for agriculture, and stated that the farther one went north the warmer the summers became. There was no doubt they were abundantly long enough to ripen wheat thoroughly. Besides the peculiar excellence of that country for cereals, he had found thousands of **acres of** crystallized salt so pure that it was used in its natural state by the Hudson Bay Co. Coal abounded in the richest veins, and was so interstratified with hematite or iron ore, yielding 50 per cent., that no locality could be better for manufacturing. Thousands of acres of coal-oil fields were found. The tar lying on the surface of the ground was ankle deep; miles and miles of the purest gypsum beds cropped out of the river banks; coal beds abounded along on the eastern slopes of the Rocky Mountains, and extended in large seams throughout the country at its base for a distance of one hundred miles. In short, Prof. Macoun believed the North-West to be the richest part of Canada, and prophesied that it would yet be the home of millions of people prosperous and happy.

An early opening of navigation on the great lakes is expected. The "first boat" at Thunder Bay is looked for about the 5th or 6th of May, more than two weeks earlier than it arrived last year.

WINNIPEG, Sept. 6th, 1876.

DEAR SIR,—in answer to your inquiries, under date Aug. 30th, I have to say:—

Government land of the first quality, prairie or wooded, can be had within 30 to 50 miles of Winnipeg and near other new settlements, with stores, church and school facilities, by every male over 18 years of age or female head of family, on the following terms, viz.:—A homestead of 160 acres, free; a pre-emption of 160 acres at $1 per acre, on a credit of 3 years; both to be partially cultivated and made a *bona fide* farm, and the homestead resided upon.

The land in the Red River valley is a rich black loam, and will average two feet in depth; it is very productive and lasting. Further west the soil is lighter and more mixed with sand. Where settled upon, as far west as 200 miles, Ontario emigrants prefer it, as being earlier and more workable, and also very productive.

New land should be broken in time to be thoroughly rotted for cultivation next year, though a great part of the crops of this year were sown on the newly broken sod, cross ploughed, but realizing only half a crop.

The degree of cold is undoubtedly greater here than in Ontario, but is drier and healthier. This season we have had a greater rainfall than for the past two years; usually our proportion is less than in Ontario, though the dews are much heavier.

Thinking farmers have come to the conclusion that one dollar per bushel for wheat in Manitoba, when the cost for fenced land, prepared for the seed, is not ten dollars per acre, and the crop is thirty to forty bushels per acre, is quite equal to one dollar and fifty cents per bushel in Ontario.

The valley of the Assiniboine, especially on its heavily wooded side, the south, is remarkable for its numerous and fine wild fruit,—plums, cherries, gooseberries, dewberries, currants, grapes, saskatoons, raspberries, strawberries, and cranberries being found at various places in great profusion. Wild hops are also exceedingly plentiful opposite the village of High Bluff, there being acres of it apparently equal to any we cultivate. Mr. Alcock, of that place, has promised a full exhibition of it at the fall show.

The attention being paid to cattle we notice, as in Sunnyside, is on the increase, and it is hoped that ere long our importation of beef will also cease. It must be remembered that incoming settlers will always require large numbers of cattle for first supply, so that a large increase must be made before a surplus is reached. Messrs. Taite, Taylor, Cunningham, Hall, Farmer, Bremner, Trestan, Clouston, Stephenson, and others have good herds to which they are rapidly making additions.

QUERIES ANSWERED.

In reply to an intending settler in Manitoba or the North-West, who writes us from Ontario, we would say :—Battleford is the future capital of the North-West Territory. The Indian title has been extinguished to the territory for hundreds of miles around that place. Battleford is about 650 miles west of Winnipeg. The land upon both the North and South Saskatchewan is good for settlement. That entire section of country is known as the Saskatchewan valley. Coal abounds there. The only practicable emigrant routes to Manitoba are open during the season of navigation by rail *via* Detroit or Port Huron and St. Paul to Moorhead, and thence by Red River steamer to Winnipeg, or by the lake steamboat to Duluth, thence by rail to Moorhead, and thence by Red River steamboat as already stated. Through tickets and full information can be obtained at most railroad and ticket offices in Ontario during the season. A first-class stage runs between Moorhead and Winnipeg all the year, which conveys the mails. First-class general purpose horses are worth from $300 to $600 per team. Agricultural implements, furniture, etc., can mostly be bought in Winnipeg to better advantage than they can be bought in Ontario and brought through by immigrants. Canadian waggons are too heavy for this country, and the ploughs are not at all adapted.

But it is · established as an indisputable fact, that wheat can be grown successfully from east to west of the Fertile Belt, and northward far down the Mackenzie River and its tributaries. In the lower parishes of Red River the yield throws all Canadian experience into the shade. The same land has been sown with wheat for fifty years, and, without being manured, has returned when unmolested by grasshoppers and floods, as much as sixty bushels to the acre. Westward, the return is from thirty to forty bushels per acre, the soil being lighter but cleaner and more easily worked than the stiff clays of Red River, and much less affected by drought. These statements may seem exaggerations to the reader, but they are literal truths and beyond contradiction. When we consider then the ease with which farming operations may be carried on in the North-West; its adaptedness to machinery, the absence of stumps or stones rendering the whole breadth of service available; and the prodigal yield; we can clearly appreciate the necessity of immediate enterprise in developing the country both by rail and water. The immediate construction of the Pacific Railway is warranted by every consideration of sound policy and public interest. Thirty years hence it will employ three lines of railway to carry the wheat of the North-West to tide-water, and all the canalling privileges which can be devised as well. For the last few years a market has been found for the surplus production of the country sufficiently remunerative amongst the Indians, from immigrants themselves, and from internal consumption. But now that immigration is likely to pour in in vastly increased volume, it will soon be necessary to provide a cheap as well as a speedy transit for grain, and to this end a water route is as necessary as a railway. The difference in cost of transport by water and by rail is in the ratio of one to three, and this difference is so immense, when taken in connection with the remote centres of production, so as to make the opening of a water route imperatively necessary. It is fortunate that we have two routes to the sea, mainly by water, and that it is not impossible to connect the Saskatchewan with Lake Superior. The development of this route would establish the greatest system of internal water communication on the continent, and the time is coming when barges will load at the foot of the Rocky Mountains and discharge cargo at Montreal; or, at all events, when there shall be but one or two transhipments between these points.—*From the Canadian Monthly.*

TOTOGAN.

From a Correspondent.

The past week has seen much done in the progress of fall ploughing, and the continued open weather seems to promise the farmers ample time for the completion of their preparations for the winter. The progress of the threshing has enabled us to obtain more accurate statistics relative to the yield of wheat; and these confirm with remarkable accuracy the estimated yield published in the FREE PRESS, a short time since. The average would have been higher had it not been for the great luxuriance of the straw in some districts, which caused it to be laid early in the season; and for the partial damage done by the birds—the latter being chiefly confined, however to the river farms, and those districts where the brush and timber predominate, being little felt on the more open prairie, where the best samples of grain have in nearly every instance been produced. A farmer in the immediate neighbourhood affirms that the yield of his wheat would have reached fully fifty bushels to the acre had the birds been less destructive; the crop under existing circumstances threshed out a net forty bushels to the acre. He has perhaps been the greatest sufferer in the vicinity from this cause.

RAINY LAKE DISTRICT.

The country immediately to the north of the Rainy River having been blocked out into townships last winter by Mr. Reed, P.L.S., is now being subdivided. A great portion fronting upon the river has been completed, and by the opening of navigation all the river frontages will have been surveyed and be opened for settlement. The surveyors report a great quantity of muskeg in the back townships, which they say can easily be drained, and will make fine farming land, little or no clearing having to be done. There is a belt of higher land upon the bank of the river, varying in depth from half to three or four miles. The whole country in rear is interspersed by low ridges, with similar land to that upon the bank of the river. These ridges, as a rule, follow the course of smaller streams, of which there are several running into the Rainy River. The soil for agricultural purposes, though not so strong as upon the prairie, is considered very good. The rapid and luxurious vegetation of wild vetches and other undergrowth never failing to astonish people who come from Ontario. I have often heard remarks passed by emigrants upon their way to Manitoba to the effect that if they had had such land as that below they would have stayed where they were. Upon the river belt and ridges, the principal growth of timber is poplar and white birch, the former attaining a size which makes it the building material of the country. It has been proved in Manitoba that poplar in a log house will last longer than oak, and I have seen several instances of old houses, thirty or forty years old, being pulled down, and the poplar logs remaining as sound as they were the day they were put there. I believe in Ontario that the growth of poplar is generally considered a bad indication for the soil. If so, that must not be taken as a criterion for this country, and it must be remembered that the prairie, whose wonderful wheat growing properties are well known, grows scarcely any other timber. Between the ridges and the muskeg proper, are generally belts of tamarac, cedar, and spruce. The length of Rainy River has hitherto been quoted at seventy-five miles, but the survey proves it to be somewhat in excess of that distance. Its average breadth is about 150 to 200 yards, taking its rise from the foot of Rainy Lake, two miles from which is situated the village and Fort Frances, and emptying into the Lake of the Woods. Its waters abound in white fish, pike, pickerel, and sturgeon; whilst in the country are to be found moose, cariboo, bear, otter, mink, marten, &c. Partridges, pin-tail grouse and prairie chicken also abound in great quantity. There are two large rivers running into it from the south, which are at present known as the upper and lower American rivers; their junctions are about twelve or sixteen miles below Fort Frances respectively. About fourteen miles from its mouth, a small river, known as the Rapid River, falls into the Rainy River, on the American side, in a pretty cascade. This is also a fine mill site, and it is said that the country in rear abounds with pine. Grasshoppers are almost unknown here; sometimes, when they are very thick in Manitoba, a strong westerly wind brings a few, but as they have to cross a large tract of wood-land and water, they never arrive in quantities sufficient to do any damage. Neither as yet have they bred here to any extent."

BEET ROOT SUGAR.

The *Monetary Times* is of opinion that the production of beet root sugar, if prosecuted upon a sufficiently large scale, could be made very profitable in Canada. A calculation is given setting forth the estimated results of the manufacture of a thousand tons of sugar beets in the States of New York and Pennsylvania, as made by an American gentleman who has given long consideration to the subject. It is as follows:—

Expenses.

1,000 tons of beets at $4 per ton............................	$4,000
Estimated cost of manufacturing at $5 per ton...	5,000
Total...	$9,000

Results.

200 tons of pulp at $2 per ton........................	$ 400
30 tons of syrup $20 per ton........................	600
60 tons of sugar at $250 per ton..................	15,000
Total results..............................	$16,000
From which deduct expenses.......................	9,000
Leaves a profit of	$7,000

Beet root sugar manufacturing will likely, at no distant day, be a question of much interest in Manitoba and the North-West, for, without doubt, our soil is immensely superior to anything upon the continent for the production of the sugar beet. Already the matter has engaged the attention of some men, and we are persuaded that if the manufacture of beet root sugar can be carried on profitably in any part of America, Manitoba, and the North-West but await the construction of railways to offer superior advantages for such an important industry.

In conclusion we would refer the intending settler to the "Descriptive Reports of Townships in Manitoba and the North-West Territories, October 31st, 1875," in which he will be able to gather a great deal of information in regard to the soil, hay, wood, and water of the Province of Manitoba. The book can be had on application to Col. Dennis, Surveyor-General, at Ottawa.

www.ingramcontent.com/pod-product-compliance
Lightning Source LLC
Chambersburg PA
CBHW031408160426
43196CB00007B/948